Politics and People

The Ordeal of Self-Government in America

POLITICS AND PEOPLE
The Ordeal of Self-Government in America

ADVISORY EDITOR
Leon Stein

EDITORIAL BOARD
James MacGregor Burns
William E. Leuchtenburg

A TALE OF
TWO CONVENTIONS

BY
WILLIAM JENNINGS BRYAN

ARNO PRESS
A New York Times Company
New York — 1974

Reprint Edition 1974 by Arno Press Inc.

Reprinted from a copy in The University
of Illinois Library

POLITICS AND PEOPLE: The Ordeal
of Self-Government in America
ISBN for complete set: 0-405-05850-0
See last pages of this volume for titles.

Manufactured in the United States of America

Library of Congress Cataloging in Publication Data

Bryan, William Jennings, 1860-1925.
  A tale of two conventions.

  (Politics and people: the ordeal of self-government
in America)
  Reprint of the ed. published by Funk & Wagnalls,
New York.
  1. Republican Party. National Convention. 15th,
Chicago, 1912. 2. Democratic Party. National Con-
vention. Baltimore, 1912. 3. Progressive Party
(Founded 1912). National Convention. 1st, Chicago,
1912. I. Title. II. Series.
JK2263 1912.B72   329'.0221   73-19136
ISBN 0-405-05860-8

A TALE OF
TWO CONVENTIONS

CANDIDATES FOR PRESIDENT AND VICE-PRESIDENT

A TALE OF TWO CONVENTIONS

BEING AN ACCOUNT OF THE REPUBLICAN AND
DEMOCRATIC NATIONAL CONVENTIONS OF
JUNE, 1912, WITH AN OUTLINE OF THE
PROGRESSIVE NATIONAL CONVENTION
OF AUGUST IN THE SAME YEAR

BY

WILLIAM JENNINGS BRYAN

WITH SELECTIONS OF NOTABLE SPEECHES, INCLUDING THOSE OF
THEODORE ROOSEVELT, MR. BRYAN, ELIHU ROOT
AND ALTON B. PARKER, EDITED BY

VIRGIL V. McNITT

ILLUSTRATED FROM CONTEMPORARY CARTOONS

FUNK & WAGNALLS COMPANY
NEW YORK AND LONDON
1912

COPYRIGHT, 1912, BY
FUNK & WAGNALLS COMPANY
(*Printed in the United States of America*)
Published September, 1912

EDITOR'S FOREWORD

MR. BRYAN AS A NEWSPAPER CORRESPONDENT

Some of the most interesting contributions to the daily press on political subjects during the campaign of 1912 were made by Mr. Bryan, who at Chicago and Baltimore represented a number of important newspapers as a special correspondent. His daily reports were published in the following papers:

The New York *World*,
Chicago *Tribune*,
Philadelphia *Bulletin*,
Boston *Globe*,
St. Louis *Post-Dispatch*,
Cleveland *Leader*,
Baltimore *American*,
Baltimore *Star*,
Pittsburgh *Post*,
Pittsburgh *Sun*,
Washington *Times*,
Cincinnati *Enquirer*,
Toledo *Blade*,
Detroit *News*,
Chicago *Journal*,
Indianapolis *Star*,
Denver *Times*,
Youngstown *Telegram*,
Dayton *News*,
Memphis *Commercial-Appeal*,
Louisville *Herald*,
Dallas *News*,
San Jose *Times*,
Kansas City *Star*,
Minneapolis *Tribune*,
Richmond *News-Leader*,
Lincoln *Journal*,
Jacksonville (Ill.) *Journal*,
Jacksonville *Courier*,
Buffalo *Times*,

Los Angeles *Tribune*,
Spokane *Spokesman-Review*,
Seattle *Times*,
San Francisco *Chronicle*,
Omaha *News*,
Springfield (Ill.) *State Register*,
Columbia *State*,
Raleigh *News and Observer*,
New Haven *Union*.

After the conventions, Mr. Bryan was urged to collect these letters and thus give his friends an opportunity to preserve them in book form. He concluded to follow the suggestion, and to include in the book important speeches, party platforms, and a selection of contemporary cartoons. It was my privilege to work with Mr. Bryan at Chicago and Baltimore, my task being to distribute his articles among the newspapers. When Mr. Bryan concluded to bring out the book, he assigned to me the work of collecting and arranging the material as here presented.

It is a matter for regret that only a few can ever witness a national convention. Mr. Bryan's friends all over the country would have been gratified, had they been present at Chicago, and seen the evidences of personal affection which came naturally from men and women of every rank as he took his place unostentatiously among reporters for the press at the Republican convention, or when he walked about the streets, or rode in street cars. Of the reception accorded him in the unfamiliar environment of a Republican National Convention a writer in the Chicago *Journal* has given an excellent account:

Hailed by his friends as the most popular man at the Republican Convention in Chicago, and greeted by the delegates themselves as the next Democratic nominee for the Presidency, William J. Bryan moved among the crowds. In search of news for articles which he will write, Mr. Bryan met and shook hands with probably more delegates than did any leader of the Republican party. Leaders and delegates alike halted in a wild scramble to shake the hand of the Commoner and whisper a few words in his ear. Scores of them renewed old acquaintanceship. Many an anxious delegate took him aside for a friendly word on the outcome of the struggle between the Taft and Roosevelt camps, but to all such inquiries Mr. Bryan had one answer: He was in Chicago seeking information from those who make up the convention, and not imparting it to them.

Mr. Bryan went about his task of gathering news like any other reporter. He visited the principal headquarters of the candidates, and took in the headquarters of various State delegations. Here and there in the lobbies and rooms he met big leaders, with whom he held whispered conversations, asking questions and making mental memoranda.

At the Roosevelt headquarters he was greeted by Senator Dixon, nominal director of the Roosevelt campaign. William B. McKinley welcomed Mr. Bryan at the Taft headquarters, and Senator Kenyon made him feel at home in the Cummins headquarters. A dozen of the Iowa delegates and their friends surrounded him at the Cummins headquarters and joined in a cheer for him, while Senator Kenyon introduced them. He and the Senator sat on a lounge in a corner of the Cummins headquarters and conversed in low tones for several minutes.

"I'm 'covering' the convention, and I want you to remember me when you have any big news to give out," said Mr. Bryan on parting. "I'm staying at the University Club, and I want you to call me up any time of the night or day." It was just the kind of talk with which the everyday convention reporter admonishes his friends many times daily.

Mr. Bryan called on Walter Houser, manager of the La Follette boom, at the Grand Pacific Hotel, and later went to the Presidential suite in the Congress Hotel, where he sent in his name to Theodore Roosevelt. He was promptly admitted to the Roosevelt rooms, the ex-President meeting him at the door.

The door was closed on the two while they talked. Mr. Bryan did not reveal the subject discust at the interview, but it may be taken for granted that he told the Colonel to call him up at the University Club if he had any news to give out.

"Do you remember attending the Republican Convention at St. Louis in 1896, Col. Bryan?" asked a newspaper man later. "You wrote your stuff in the office of the St. Louis *Chronicle,* at a desk right next to mine. The Democratic Convention was to be held in Chicago the next week, and I can remember very well how Col. McMurray walked up and asked you who would be nominated by the Democrats. You answered very quickly: 'I haven't the slightest idea.' And the next week you were nominated yourself."

"Well," broke in Mr. Bryan, with a broad smile, "we must distinguish between ideas and hopes."

Mr. Bryan said good-by to the group after joking with them about the way he was delayed a half hour by interviewers and photographers after his arrival in the city.

"They just cornered me and I couldn't do a thing," he said: "I don't think it was right, because we fellows ought to do all we can to help one another."

He rode in an elevator to the ground floor of the Congress.

"There's Col. Bryan," said a Texas delegate to a companion. "He's writing the convention for the *Chicago Journal*. Col. Bryan, I want to shake hands with you. This is my neighbor from Texas. We are Roosevelt delegates here, and are glad to see you. This is my wife, too, Col. Bryan. She always has wanted to meet you."

At every step he was stopped by men who knew him, mostly men wearing badges of delegates. They shook his hand, inquired about his health, and that of his family, and asked his opinion of the outcome.

"Just on the quiet," was the general plea, but Mr. Bryan shook his head and answered kindly, "Wait until about next Friday, and then I'll give a prognostication as to who the next Republican candidate for President will be."

"There's Bill Bryan," or "There goes Bryan," were the words of nearly every man or woman who passed Mr. Bryan on his walk from the door of the Congress to the door of the Auditorium across the street. Arrived at the latter hotel, he went to the rooms of the Associated Press and asked for old friends, among them Melville E. Stone. Mr. Stone was out, but Mr. Bryan was careful to have his secretary make a note to the effect that W. J. Bryan had called and wished to be remembered to him.

He then sought out the headquarters of the California delegation. The room was filled with Roosevelt men, and a dozen of them made a dash for Mr. Bryan as soon as he was recognized.

"Isn't this Col. Bryan?" shouted one of the delegates, excitedly. "Why, bless me, boy, let me introduce you all. Col. Bryan, we're going to nominate Roosevelt at this Republican Convention, and we hope he won't have to run against you. I'm not afraid of a single other Democrat."

"Very nice of you to say so," said Mr. Bryan. "But I'm not a candidate to-day. I'm a reporter. I'd like to see Governor Johnson if I may."

The secretary said that Mr. Johnson was in a very important conference, but he felt that the Governor would adjourn the conference to be interviewed by such a distinguished reporter. While the secretary was gone to notify the Governor, Mr. Bryan shook hands with Benjamin Ide Wheeler, president of the University of California, with whom he discust a number of subjects. From the corridor a crowd swept into the headquarters and gathered around the two, and soon Mr. Bryan was talking loud enough to be heard by a dozen or more of those around him. He ended the talk with, "Well, I've learned the great lesson of patience."

Mr. Bryan was thanking the two graciously when Governor Johnson arrived from his conference. He greeted Mr. Bryan warmly, and, with President Wheeler and others, the two looked over the hotel balcony out onto Lake Michigan and discussed generalities. Mr. Bryan related how he had used a California flag which President Wheeler had sent him to decorate his daughter's rooms at his Lincoln, Neb., home.

Finally he put his arm around Governor Johnson's shoulder and whispered that he wanted a word with him. The two retired to chairs in the corner of the rooms and discust the convention situation earnestly for more than twenty minutes. Evidently they were old friends.

While they were talking the group of delegates enlarged.

"What do you know about the Governor being interviewed by Bryan?" said one of them.

"He's the best of the lot," said another. "I'd rather see him run than the whole bunch," not elucidating whether he included his idol, Teddy, in the "bunch."

"Well, there's one thing certain," said a Colorado man who had come in. "Roosevelt can carry Colorado if he runs on a baggage ticket. Next to him, Bryan is the most popular man in Colorado."

From the California rooms Mr. Bryan hastened to the New York headquarters.

"I want to see Fred Tanner," he told the doortender. Mr. Tanner was found. He evidently appreciated the honor of a call. They greeted one another warmly. It turned out that Mr. Tanner is Frederick C., the son of Edward A. Tanner, former president of the Illinois College at Jacksonville, Ill., who married Mr. and Mrs. Bryan. The Tanners and the Bryans were next-door neighbors. Mr. Bryan had read that the younger Tanner was a delegate from New York and so looked him up.

"Fred," he said, "I'm writing some things about this convention, and I want you to remember me if you get any news that you want printed. Call me up at the University Club, and see that I don't get scooped on the New York news."

Mr. Tanner introduced the Colonel to a dozen or more Taft delegates who were in the room.

"Colonel," said one of the men, "is it possible that we shall have the pleasure of voting for you in the fall if Mr. Taft is not nominated?"

"I'll tell you," responded Mr. Bryan. "I'm in the position of the man who was met in the street by a friend who asked him if he could change a $10 bill. 'No,' replied the man, 'but I appreciate the compliment just the same.'"

"If Roosevelt is nominated and you run in the fall," said another Taft delegate, "I have heard many Republicans say that you will carry New York State by a big vote."

"I was told that twice before," Mr. Bryan answered, with his broadest smile and a pat on the back.

At Baltimore the circumstances were different. Here Mr. Bryan was in the house of political friends and a cordial reception was inevitable. Here as at Chicago Mr. Bryan acted as a newspaper reporter. He was also a delegate, and not only that, but he became the most active and potent personal force in the convention. Many experienced political observers have declared that the fortunes of the day were determined by him. Friends of Mr. Bryan would have been thrilled by his eloquence in Baltimore. It was put forth in the midst of his newspaper activities and in the face of seemingly desperate odds on the floor of the convention. These battles day after day were often fought against the advice of timid friends. These friends hung their heads in trepidation as storms of anger and abuse raged about him. It was a wonderful struggle, and particularly so because Mr. Bryan won it so decisively, in spite of the utmost efforts of a hostile majority, bent upon defeating a man whose high purposes they could not understand.

The printed page cannot supply the color, the action or the din of the encounter; it merely offers so much as can be preserved. While it may lack some of the gripping qualities of the actual scenes, it at any rate will afford means for a more careful analysis of measures and motives than could have been made at the time of the convention itself.

VIRGIL V. MCNITT.

AUGUST 12, 1912.

CONTENTS

	PAGE
Editor's Foreword—Mr. Bryan as a Newspaper Correspondent	v
Introduction	xxi
By Mr. Bryan.	

PART I.

THE REPUBLICAN NATIONAL CONVENTION

Chicago, June 18-22, 1912

I.	The Preliminary Skirmishing	3
	Mr. Bryan's first letter, in morning newspapers of Monday, June 17.	
II.	The Opposing Leaders—A Study of Types	10
	Mr. Bryan's letter in afternoon newspapers of Monday, June 17.	
III.	Just Before the Battle	15
	Mr. Bryan's letter in morning newspapers of Tuesday, June 18.	
IV.	The Roosevelt Mass Meeting at the Auditorium	22
	Mr. Bryan's letter in afternoon newspapers of Tuesday, June 18.	

CONTENTS

		PAGE
V.	How Elihu Root Was Chosen Temporary Chairman	29
	Mr. Bryan's letter in morning newspapers of Wednesday, June 19.	
VI.	An Analysis of the Chairmanship Contest	37
	Mr. Bryan's letter in afternoon newspapers of Wednesday, June 19.	
VII.	The Roosevelt-Hadley Demonstration	44
	Mr. Bryan's letter in morning newspapers of Thursday, June 20.	
VIII.	The Futility of the Demonstration.	53
	Mr. Bryan's letter in afternoon newspapers of Thursday, June 20.	
IX.	On the Eve of the Crisis	61
	Mr. Bryan's letter in morning newspapers of Friday, June 21.	
X.	The Convention as a Photograph of the Nation	66
	Mr. Bryan's letter in afternoon newspapers of Friday, June 21.	
XI.	California's Day	72
	Mr. Bryan's letter in morning newspapers of Saturday, June 22.	

		PAGE
XII.	The Day Before the Last	77
	Mr. Bryan's letter in afternoon newspapers of Saturday, June 22.	
XIII.	The End of the Convention	82
	Mr. Bryan's letter in morning newspapers of Sunday, June 23.	
	Withdrawal of the Roosevelt Delegates	85
	Speech of Henry J. Allen and Statement of Mr. Roosevelt....	85
XIV.	The Republican Platform	90
XV.	A Criticism of Mr. Taft's Speech of Acceptance	99
	Mr. Bryan's article in morning newspapers of August 3.	

Part II

THE DEMOCRATIC NATIONAL CONVENTION

Baltimore, June 25-July 2, 1912

I.	The Two Contending Factions	109
	Mr. Bryan's letter in morning newspapers of Monday, June 24.	
II.	The Fight for a Progressive Chairman	116

CONTENTS

		PAGE
	Mr. Bryan's letter in afternoon newspapers of Monday, June 24.	
III.	The Steam Roller at Work	121
	Mr. Bryan's letter in morning newspapers of Tuesday, June 25.	
IV.	Financial Interests at Work	126
V.	Alton B. Parker Made Temporary Chairman	127
	Mr. Bryan's letter in morning newspapers of Wednesday, June 26.	
	Speech of Mr. Bryan Opposing the Election of Alton B. Parker	134
	Speech of Senator Kern; a Plea for Harmony	142
VI.	An Amazing Spectacle in the Convention	146
	Mr. Bryan's letter in afternoon newspapers of Wednesday, June 26.	
VII.	The Tide Turns	152
	Mr. Bryan's letter in morning newspapers of Thursday, June 27.	
VIII.	Bossism Becomes the Issue	158
	Mr. Bryan's letter in afternoon newspapers of Thursday, June 27.	

CONTENTS

		PAGE
IX.	The Anti-Morgan-Ryan-Belmont Resolution	162
	Mr. Bryan's letter in morning newspapers of Friday, June 28.	
X.	The Adoption of the Resolution	167
	Mr. Bryan's letter in afternoon newspapers of Friday, June 28.	
	Mr. Bryan's Speech on the Resolution	172
	The Candidates Discussed	175
XI.	Awaiting the Nomination	180
	Mr. Bryan's letter in morning newspapers of Saturday, June 29.	
XII.	The Money Trust's Activities	184
	Mr. Bryan's letter in afternoon newspapers of Saturday, June 29.	
XIII.	How Votes Were Changed	187
	Mr. Bryan's letter in morning newspapers of Monday, July 1.	
	Mr. Bryan's Speech Explaining His Vote	193
XIV.	The Close of the Convention	198
	Mr. Bryan's letter in morning newspapers of Wednesday, July 3.	
	Mr. Bryan's Valedictory	203
	An Interview with Mr. Bryan	206
XV.	The Democratic Platform	208

		PAGE
XVI.	Governor Wilson's Speech of Acceptance	228
	Mr. Bryan's comments as published on August 9	228
XVII.	The Influence of Mr. Bryan in the Convention	236
	Some of the comments on it by leading newspapers	238

Part III

THE PROGRESSIVE NATIONAL CONVENTION

Chicago, August 5-7, 1912

I.	A Summary of Events	247
II.	Mr. Roosevelt's Speech in the Convention	250
III.	The Platform	279
IV.	Comments on the Progressive Party. Mr. Bryan's Article published in newspapers of Saturday, August 10	296

LIST OF CARTOONS

		PAGE
1.	The Education of Willie Bryan (As a newspaper correspondent at the Republican Convention.)	4
2.	At the Republican Convention—Mr. Bryan Enjoying the Discussion	30
3.	Mr. Bryan's Departure from the Republican Convention	86
4.	Atlas	111
5.	Trying to Square it With the Peerless Leader	123
6.	Convention Studies	130
7.	William Jennings Bryan Draws a Cartoon	149
8.	Mr. Bryan's Cartoon—Another Representation	150
9.	Mr. Bryan's Second Cartoon	151
10.	The Baltimore Transformation	155
11.	The Sacrifice Hit	190
12.	The Candidate We All Support	305

INTRODUCTION

TWO EPOCH-MAKING CONVENTIONS

Criticism of men is only useful when it leads to reforms, and criticism of conventions is only worth uttering or reading when attention is called to errors that can be corrected.

The Chicago Convention gave in an exaggerated form an object-lesson that seemed necessary to awaken the public to evils that have existed for years. The two evils that stood out prominently at Chicago were, first, the organization of a new convention by an old, outgrown committee; and, second, the employment, for the purpose of overriding a majority of committeemen, of delegations representing mythical constituencies in the South.

It has been customary in all parties for the committee which conducts a campaign to retain its authority until the next convention is permanently organized. In ordinary times the power thus conferred upon an old committee is not misused, but in times of upheaval and change the power is subject to abuse. It was abused in the Democratic convention at Chicago in 1896 when an old committee, friendly to the administration, undertook to control a new convention antagonistic to the administration.

Likewise at the Republican convention, held at Chicago this year, a considerable number of the committeemen had been repudiated in their own States and acted contrary to the known wishes of their successors on the committee and the delegations from those States. As the new committeemen do not begin to serve until the permanent organization is perfected, the old committee is able to determine the character of the new convention.

Something over two hundred and fifty delegates were contested before the national committee and the Taft men were seated in nearly every case. More than two-thirds of these contests were dropt and only about seventy-five taken before the convention, but the seventy-five were enough to determine the complexion of the convention. If the seventy-five Roosevelt delegates were seated it would make it a Roosevelt convention; if the seventy-five Taft delegates were seated it would put the Taft forces in control. The old national committee, holding over from four years ago, had the right according to custom to make up the temporary roll-call and it gave the seventy-five Taft men seats in the convention. These Taft delegates voted on the contests that came before the convention. Of course, each delegate was prohibited

INTRODUCTION

from voting in his own case, but the contests were decided in small groups, and while a delegate could not vote in his own case, he could vote in all the other cases, and, as the contested delegates understood that they must stand or fall together, the effect was just the same as if each man had voted to seat himself.

The old committee was able to, and in fact did, decide the issue between the two contending factions. It is not for me to say that the Taft committee ignored justice and equity in those decisions—that is a question which I am glad to leave the Republicans to decide. Neither is it for me to say that a Roosevelt committee would not have acted on the same principle adopted by the Taft men if Mr. Roosevelt's faction had controlled the committee. I would not even say that a Democratic committee would have acted differently—I have known Democratic committeemen to be just as willing to use their power to advance their own side of a contest. My contention is that frail human beings ought not to be subjected to the temptations presented at Chicago and in other conventions. When a presidential nomination is at stake and the course of a four years' administration is involved in a decision, a great many men who are thoroughly honest and, when disinterested, very just, yield to the temptation to put the end above the means to the extent of employing means that they cannot defend to secure an end which they regard as of great importance. The members of the Tilden-Hayes electoral commission—all noted men—did this in 1877. The question is not whether the Taft men were worse than Roosevelt men or what Democrats would have been under similar circumstances, but whether the system can be so reformed as to remove such powerful temptations.

The Baltimore platform suggests the selection of national committeemen by popular vote; this is an improvement over the old method of selection by the national delegates. But what is more important, the Baltimore platform advocates a revolutionary change when it suggests that the *new committeemen begin to serve as soon as elected.* This creates a new committee in sympathy with the new convention and puts an end to the evils that arise from the action of a hold-over committee, made up in part of committeemen already repudiated in their own States. If this rule had been in force in the Chicago convention the Roosevelt faction would have been much stronger in the national committee. This change, however, could not have been made at the convention, because the delegates would have considered the immediate effects of the change rather than the merits of the change itself, but now that the matter can be passed upon deliberately and dispassionately it is quite certain that the

Baltimore proposal will commend itself to fair-minded men of all parties.

The second difficulty, namely, the imaginary constituency, is one that is peculiar to the Republican situation and has no counterpart in a Democratic convention. While a number of the States are generally Republican, still the Democratic party in these States is a real force and there is no reason why the Democrats of the Republican States should not enjoy full participation in the writing of platforms and in the making of nominations.

In the case of the Republican party, however, it is different. In a number of the southern States the Republican party is a fiction. It exerts no approachable influence in local affairs and is held together by prospect of federal patronage. Take the State of Mississippi, for instance. It had twenty delegates in the Republican convention in Chicago and these twenty delegates voted quite consistently to carry out the Taft program. There were at the last presidential election only 4,505 votes—Republican votes—in Mississippi, while in my district in Nebraska, the first district, there were 18,642 votes. The first district of Nebraska had two delegates in the Chicago convention, and, as one of the six districts of Nebraska, it joined in the selection of four at large, its proportionate strength being a little less than three delegates, or less than one-sixth as many as Mississippi had, and yet it cast more than four times as many votes as the Republican party cast in the State of Mississippi. In other words, the average Mississippi Republican had twenty-four times as much influence in the Chicago convention as the average Republican in the first district of Nebraska. I only take Mississippi as an illustration. The same thing is true in Louisiana, in South Carolina, in Alabama, and to a less degree in a number of other southern States.

This disproportionate representation has existed for some time and has more than once scandalized the proceedings of Republican conventions. Now that public attention has been turned upon the situation. I have so much faith in the intelligence and patriotism of the rank and file of the Republican party that I feel sure some remedy will be found to the end that the Republican conventions hereafter may represent the voters of the Republican party. Republicans can decide for themselves whether their party's interests would have been advanced better by the nomination of Mr. Taft or by the nomination of Mr. Roosevelt, but when the interests of candidates are put aside and the question is viewed upon its merits no considerable portion of the Republican party will seriously advocate the continuance of a system by which a minority either in the organization or in the convention can stifle the voice of a majority of the party.

The unit rule was the main cause of difficulty at Baltimore. It ought to be abolished and all delegates, except the four at large, ought to be selected by districts, as Republican delegates are selected.

Looking upon convention proceedings from the standpoint of one desiring improvement along every line I feel that the two great conventions of 1912, the Republican national convention at Chicago and the Democratic national convention at Baltimore, will prove epoch-making because of the reforms that will result from them.

The chief lesson taught by the Baltimore convention was quite a different lesson from that taught at Chicago. It shows as no former convention has done the power of public opinion. The pressure brought to bear upon the Baltimore convention by "the Democrats at home" is a signal illustration of the fact that representative government is a fact in the United States. No plan of misrepresentation, whether intentional or unintentional, is likely to succeed when it becomes known. Governments throughout the world are becoming more and more responsive to the will of the people, and our own government is becoming increasingly sensitive to the wishes of the voters. The selection of Judge Parker for temporary chairman was a challenge to the progressive element of the party and the manner in which the challenge was accepted shows how sound the party is at heart.

The anti-Morgan-Ryan-Belmont resolution would have been voted down by a considerable majority but for the fact that the delegates feared the wrath that a negative vote would have aroused at home. And so, in the concluding hours of the convention, an alliance with Mr. Murphy and with the interests which he represented in the convention became more and more a thing to be feared as the telegrams poured in from forty-eight States.

This "Tale of Two Conventions" is given in the hope that the facts set forth will be helpful to the American people in the understanding of public questions. Both conventions were turbulent, but truth emerges triumphant from every contest. There is no real contradiction between the two propositions: first, that truth is the cause of revolutions; and, second, that truth is a peacemaker. Truth combats error and does not retire from the contest until error is overthrown, but truth is a peacemaker in the end, because nothing can be permanent that does not rest upon truth.

The casual observer may be carried away by the exciting incidents of a convention, but the sober citizen will see in a national convention a great human agency for the accomplishment of an important end. Our conventions will cease to be interesting only when nothing remains to be accomplished.

WILLIAM JENNINGS BRYAN.

Part One

THE REPUBLICAN NATIONAL CONVENTION
CHICAGO, JUNE 18-22, 1912

I

THE PRELIMINARY SKIRMISHING

Mr. Bryan's first letter, published in morning newspapers of Monday, June 17th.

Chicago, June 16.—There is a liberal education in a national convention, but much that one learns is not useful to him afterwards. Nowhere else does one see in full bloom this special phase of convention life that politics develops in a free country. The headquarters of the various candidates are in charge of skilful politicians enlisted under the respective banners, and these have their assistants and understudies who are in training.

The delegates as they come in are badged, tagged and buttonholed. The prophets are revising their lists as they learn of additions or defections and the corridors of the hotels resound with the cheers of partisans. These things are to be found in every convention, but they are here in unusual abundance.

The Republican party contains a larger number of prominent and experienced politicians than are

THE EDUCATION OF WILLIE BRYAN.
(*As a Newspaper Correspondent at the Republican Convention.*)
Bart, in the Minneapolis "Journal."

THE REPUBLICAN CONVENTION

to be found in the Democratic party, for prominence usually goes hand in hand with official positions. For the last half century, the Republican party has been in almost uninterrupted control of the nation and has been supreme in a majority of the States. It has had an opportunity, therefore to lift its members into conspicuous positions.

As one passes through the increasing throng he hears men addressed as "governor," "senator," and "secretary," until he becomes bewildered at the array of officials now holding offices or with the prefix "ex" before their titles—a prefix which courtesy drops in salutation.

I am enjoying my first day renewing acquaintance with the adherents of the various candidates and with the numerous representatives of the press. I called upon Representative McKinley* at the Taft headquarters, upon Senator Dixon† at the Roosevelt headquarters, upon Senator Kenyon at the Cummins headquarters, and upon Mr. Houser at Senator La Follette's headquarters. I am now trying to reconcile the predictions that they make.

At the Taft headquarters the President is as good as renominated. He has the necessary votes and can read his title clear. There may be a varia-

* Manager of the Taft forces in the convention.
† Manager of the Roosevelt forces.

tion of a few votes, but the margin is sufficient so that a few desertions—not anticipated, of course, but allowed for out of an abundance of caution—would not change the result.

This would seem to settle the question in favor of Mr. Taft, but for the fact that a different story is told at the Roosevelt headquarters. Here it is all over but the shouting, and even that has been entered upon.

With the ex-President's followers the exact number of votes is not so important, because they feel that they have on their side a sentiment that will compel additions. They are banking on the fact that Mr. Roosevelt has a majority of the votes from the northern States, where the Republican vote is located, and they are using this argument for all it is worth. They will not admit there is any doubt as to the final outcome.

After one has visited these two headquarters he feels that while the issue is in doubt between the President and the ex-President, the choice must lie between the two, but Senator Kenyon and Mr. Houser have carefully prepared tables which show that neither of the principal candidates can be nominated, and that in a long drawn out contest, such as they expect, the party must turn to some third person, and each thinks his candidate the logical man for the place.

I am not prepared to venture a prediction; in

fact, no one who views the subject impartially would care to risk a guess. The predictions that are being made by interested parties illustrate the old truth that man's opinion of what is to be is half wish and half environment.

Senator Kenyon wants it distinctly understood that Senator Cummins will not consider the vice presidency in connection with either President Taft, ex-President Roosevelt, or anybody else. Those in charge of Mr. La Follette's candidacy are equally emphatic in denying that they have any intention of taking sides with either Mr. Roosevelt or Mr. Taft.

I called on Mr. Roosevelt and found him cheerful and as buoyant as I have ever seen him. Opinion differs as to the effect of his presence here.* His opponents think that his personal participation in the convention is so unusual a manifestation of interest as to offset any good that he can do. His friends, on the other hand, are cheered by the audacity of his course. They are counting on his strengthening any wavering friends, as well as upon his winning over any opponents who are not riveted to the Taft candidacy.

The X, or unknown quantity, in the Republican situation is the colored vote from the South. It is the weakness of the Taft cause. It is a weakness

* An avowed leading candidate is believed never before to have attended a presidential convention.

not only because it does not represent a voting strength proportionate to its influence in the convention but a weakness also because it cannot be depended upon to stand tied.

There is a break in the Mississippi delegation and another in the Georgia delegation. One of the Mississippi delegates has returned some money which was given to him for traveling expenses for the delegates, but there are Taft supporters who are uncharitable enough to charge that this money would not have been returned had not a larger sum been received from "sources unknown."

In fact, it looks now as if this convention might turn on the size of the "honorarium," as the magazines describe the complimentary compensation paid to those who write for them.

A Western senator used to tell at Washington a story that does not seem as absurd now as it did then. He used it to show the honesty of some of the Western legislators. One of them arose in the State legislature during a senatorial contest and thus addressed the speaker:

"I have received $1,000 from Mr. ——— (we will call him Mr. Smith), and I intended to vote for him for senator, but since receiving the money and promising him my support I have received $1,500 from Mr. ——— (we will call him Mr. Brown), and, being an honest man, I desire to return Mr. Smith's money."

It is unfortunate that the forces are so evenly divided as to make it possible for the scale to be turned by influences which would deprive the victor of the right to claim a real triumph for the principles for which he stands.

II

THE OPPOSING LEADERS—A STUDY OF TYPES

Mr. Bryan's letter in afternoon newspapers of Monday, June 17th.

Chicago, June 17.—One notes a difference in the manner and bearing of delegates as they come pouring into the city and report at their respective headquarters. The Taft men, excepting the Southern delegates, are as a rule of the conservative type. They speak more deliberately and show less animation. Many of them are politicians of long experience who have been accustomed to the methods of the inner circle. They speak cautiously, act deliberately, and are more inclined to "view with alarm" than to enthuse. They feel that things have been going along fairly well, and are anxious that such changes as are necessary may be made "slowly and only after careful investigation." The Roosevelt men, on the contrary, are largely of the aggressive type. They have already decided matters and have no doubts to settle. They are not waiting for investigation and are not weighing reforms in apothecary scales.

A great many young men have come into prominence as Roosevelt champions. Some of them appear younger than they really are. Gov. Johnson, of California, is the most interesting figure from the west. His state, so long a victim of railroad rule and servitude to favor-seeking corporations, has leapt at one bound into the front rank of reform States. With the zeal of a new convert California points with pride to an army of militant progressives, and only awaits the signals to fight Standpatism on any field. Stubbs, of Kansas; Hadley, of Missouri, and Aldrich, of Nebraska, are untiring workers and they don't talk in whispers.

While the personality of Mr. Roosevelt is a considerable factor in the contest, it is evident from what one hears that the progressive Republicans are using Mr. Roosevelt not because they approve of all that he stands for, but because they regard him as the best means of overthrowing the Taft régime. They regard the President as the personification of reactionary sentiment in the nation and would support almost any one in preference to him. Some of them admit that the anti-third term argument is a handicap, but feel that it is not a sufficient objection to deter them from casting in their lot with the ex-President. I cannot agree with them in putting this objection aside so lightly. It has not yet been considered by the public.

President Taft is not in a position to urge the

strongest objections to a third term, and the sharp line drawn between the administration and its opponents precludes a fair discussion of the third-term issue. If Mr. Roosevelt should be pitted against a progressive Democrat there would be better opportunity to give weight to the objections which are honestly and earnestly advanced.

The unfortunate phase of the controversy is that discussion of an issue so fundamental would turn attention from the economic questions upon which the people seem ready to act. That this would be the result of Mr. Roosevelt's nomination is certain.

Had he espoused the cause of any other progressive and given to it the time and energy that he has devoted to his own candidacy he could have controlled the convention and made himself master of the organization of his party. The bitterness aroused by his candidacy would have been avoided and his party would have been committed to the reforms for which the progressives stand. The Democratic party then would have had a rival that would have spurred it on to even greater activity in support of remedial measures.

But there is time enough to philosophize on what might have been. The question just now is, how many Taft delegates can the Roosevelt leaders, aided by the ex-President himself, draw from the President's fold?

The desertions claimed at the Roosevelt headquarters are discredited by Mr. McKinley. It is conceded that a Mississippi delegate, heretofore counted for Mr. Taft, has joined the Roosevelt forces, and that one of the Georgia delegates has followed his example, but the standpatters expect that the effect of these desertions will be reduced to a minimum by a discussion of considerations which are supposed to have brought about the changes.

While the charges made in former Republican conventions against some of the colored delegates have prepared the public mind to accept without much evidence the charge that money is being used it must be remembered that the patronage argument has a powerful influence on whites as well as blacks. The most powerful weapon in the Roosevelt armory is the argument that Mr. Taft cannot possibly be elected and cannot therefore reward his delegates in the Southern States. Mr. Roosevelt's friends take it for granted that he can win, and their confidence in his success enables them to play upon the ambitions of delegates, especially in the Democratic states where the Republicans cannot hope for local offices.

While a goodly sum in the hand is worth two offices in the bush, both inducements must be taken into calculation in a contest like that now being waged for supremacy in the party.

The fight over the temporary chairmanship seems

likely to give the first reliable indication of the line-up and it may be left to the followers of La Follette and Cummins to decide the question, provided they are willing to take the responsibility, but they may prefer to withhold their votes rather than be counted with either side.

Neutrality is their strong card and they would find it difficult to support the candidate of either side without subjecting themselves to misrepresentation.

The Roosevelt meeting to-night will give opportunity for an outburst of enthusiasm, and as the ex-President is going to speak it is safe to predict that he will studiously refrain from praising the Republican national committee. In fact, he may brush up on the criminal law and make some additions to the list of adjectives which he has already employed in describing the various forms of larceny which he has charged against his opponent.

The war goes merrily on, and I feel even more than a journalistic interest in watching it.

III

JUST BEFORE THE BATTLE

Mr. Bryan's letter in morning newspapers of Tuesday, June 18th.

Chicago, June 17.—It is "just before the battle, mother." The writer is able to survey the scene more calmly than those who "may be numbered with the slain." The feeling, as one meets with it in the corridors of hotels, is not as bitter as some of the expressions of some of the delegates would indicate. The lines are closely drawn and each side is putting forth its best efforts, but there is, withal, a good deal of cheerfulness, and I am trying to cultivate it wherever I can.

I am urging both sides not to take the matter too seriously, assuring them that we can correct at Baltimore any mistakes they may be unfortunate enough to make—four years from now, if not now. I find that none of them is disposed to question a Democratic victory four years ahead, and many of them are willing to admit confidentially that the Republican party is in such a muddle that the Democrats now have the chance of a lifetime.

The day closed with the Roosevelt meeting at the Auditorium, Senator Borah presiding. Both the Chairman and the ex-President were greeted with great enthusiasm, the applause lasting some minutes when Mr. Roosevelt was upon the platform. The Arabs are said to have seven hundred words which mean "camel"; Mr. Roosevelt has nearly as many synonyms for theft, and he used them all tonight. His denunciation of the National Committee was scathing, and he included the President and Senator Root in his denunciation.

The most spontaneous approval of the evening greeted his statement that the action of the convention would not be binding upon any Republican in the convention, or outside of it, if it depended upon the votes of the seventy-six delegates whose seats are to be contested before the Credentials Committee. He demands that the contested delegates shall stand aside—that is, both contested and contesting delegates—and leave the thousand uncontested delegates to decide the contest. This will evidently be the line of battle in the convention.

The latter part of the speech was an eloquent indorsement of progressive ideas and sounded so much like Senator La Follette's speeches during the last eight years and like Democratic speeches during the last sixteen years that one could hardly believe it was being applauded by a Republican audience. Only one thing was lacking to complete it; namely, a quotation from the ninth verse of the twentieth chapter of Matthew.*

The fight opens to-morrow with the election of Temporary Chairman, and an expectant audience will fill the Coliseum before noon, the opening hour. Senator Root is the choice of the Taft forces, while Senator Borah will receive the Roosevelt vote. If any one attempts to give in advance of the roll call the actual number of votes to be cast for each he will be walking "by faith rather than by sight." It is likely that the La Follette and Cummins delegates will withhold their votes rather than cast them for either candidate.

As both Cummins and La Follette must receive votes from both sides in order to win the Presidential prize their friends are disposed to avoid an alliance actual, or even seeming, with either group. As Taft and Roosevelt have nearly equal strength and together control more than nine-tenths of the convention, the other candidates can afford to let them fight out their differences and await the result.

As soon as the temporary organization is completed the Committee on Credentials will be announced, and the struggle which was begun before the National Committee will be renewed. The

* See Mr. Bryan's letter, dated June 18, for this quotation.

Roosevelt forces will have a larger representation on the Credentials Committee than they had on the National Committee, and about eighty contests will be submitted to this committee. The remaining contests will be abandoned, and the Taft delegates will be permitted to occupy seats without further controversy. This is regarded by the President's followers as a vindication of the fairness of the committee, but the ex-President's friends reply that these delegates were seated by a unanimous vote in the committee and that acquiescence on the part of the Roosevelt members of the National Committee is proof of their desire to see justice done.

The eighty contests, however, are sufficient in number to decide the Presidential nomination; so that interest in the results of committee deliberations is acute. The California contest, while it involves only two delegates, has aroused more heat than some of the others of greater numerical importance. I have taken pains to consult the leaders of both parties in order to present the issue accurately.

The Taft side relies upon the wording of the call of the National Committee, which is in conformity with the rules which have governed Republican National Conventions for thirty years. According to this call the several States are permitted to introduce certain variations in the rules to conform to State law, but this permission concludes with the words "but, provided, further, that in no State shall an election be so held to prevent the delegates from any Congressional district and their alternates being selected by the Republican electors of that district."

This provision, taken in connection with the custom that has prevailed and the practice of other States, would give the Taft side a prima facie case, and they would also have the moral support of those who oppose the unit rule as unfair. It was the injustice made possible under the unit rule that led the Republican party to adopt, in 1880, the system of electing all the delegates by districts, except the four from the State at large.

As this same question is likely to come before the Baltimore Convention an illustration of what is possible under the unit rule may not be out of place. Let us use the present contest as an illustration. There are something over a thousand delegates in the Republican Convention. Let us, for convenience, fix the number at a thousand. Suppose, further, that Mr. Taft carried a majority of the districts in States electing 500 delegates, and that Mr. Roosevelt carried a majority of the districts electing a remainder of 500 delegates. If, where Mr. Taft had a majority, his friends invoked the unit rule and gave him the entire 500 votes, while Mr. Roosevelt's friends did not resort to this rule, Mr. Taft would have 500 votes plus nearly

250, while Mr. Roosevelt would have only a few more than 250.

In the case supposed the use of the unit rule would give the one who employed it an unfair advantage over the one who did not employ it. The unit rule, to be fair, ought to be used in all the States, and even then injustice is possible under it. In the California case, however, the Roosevelt men are not compelled to rely entirely on the general arguments advanced in behalf of the unit rule. They insist, first, that the primary law of California substitutes a system of election by the State at large for the district system when certain formalities were complied with, and they contend that the formalities were complied with in this case. The law supersedes the language employed in the committee's call. In the second place, they declare that the Taft delegates, who now claim election in the district, were candidates before the State at large and became so with the indorsement of President Taft, thus being stopped from questioning the validity of the election of their opponents.

In addition to these contentions the Roosevelt men argue that there is no possible way of determining the exact vote in the Fourth District, the district in controversy, because fourteen precincts are partly in that district and partly in the Fifth District. The vote between Roosevelt and Taft in the Fourth District was so close that the votes of these fourteen precincts would change the result, but no one is able to say how many of those living on the Fourth District side of the line running through the fourteen precincts voted for Tāft and how many for Roosevelt.

IV

THE ROOSEVELT MASS MEETING AT THE AUDITORIUM

Mr. Bryan's letter in afternoon newspapers of Tuesday, June 18th.

Chicago, June 18.—As this letter must necessarily be put upon the wires before the convention convenes at noon I shall devote it to the most interesting and only significant event of yesterday, namely, the Roosevelt mass meeting at the Auditorium in the evening.

The hall was filled with ticket holders, and a large crowd outside mourned their lack of influence with those who were distributing the passports to the meeting. It was a boomers' meeting, and none of the accessories usual on such occasions was omitted. Flags were distributed to the audience, patriotic hymns were sung, and a glee club assured the audience that they wanted "Teddy."

Senator Borah presided and opened the meeting with a well-delivered arraignment of the National Committee and of standpat Republicanism in general. His splendid voice rang out through the large hall, and what he said pleased the audience.

He is another representative of the younger generation and has fairly won the distinction that has been accorded him of representing the progressives in the fight over the temporary chairmanship.

He will be remembered as the chairman of the committee which succeeded in forcing through the Senate the amendment providing for the popular election of Senators, an amendment which the Senate had six times refused to consider during the past twenty years. He is a conspicuous member of the group of young men referred to yesterday, which includes, besides those heretofore mentioned, Gov. Bass, of New Hampshire; Senator Dixon, ex-Secretary Garfield, Gifford Pinchot, Judge Lindsey, ex-Senator Beveridge, the junior Washburn of Minnesota, and men like Hale and Hill of Massachusetts.

It would be interesting to know just how many of these progressive Republicans are attending their first National Convention. Only one of the California delegates has attended a convention before and only one of the New Jersey delegates.

Mr. Roosevelt's speech might be described as a characteristic speech, in that he expressed himself in emphatic language and accompanied his words with gestures equally emphatic. His manner indicated that he was enjoying the fight, and the more vehement his denunciation the more vigorous the applause.

He condemned the members of the National Committee jointly and severally, individually and in groups. He described them by naming characteristics, discussed them biographically, and singled them out by name. He analyzed them in their representative character and in their lack of character. The words "theft," "crime," "stolen," "shame," "treason" and other severities of the kind were interwoven with the names of Senators, ex-Senators, bosses, ex-bosses leaders, ex-leaders and "sure-thing" men.

The response most frequently made by the audience when he asked their opinion of the action of the National Committee was the word "rotten." His main charge against the committee was that it had, as the representative of the special interests, deliberately defrauded the rank and file of the party of the fruits of victory in nearly forty districts. He divided the committee of fifty into three groups. From fifteen to twenty were included in a group to which he ascribed varying degrees of honesty.

Fourteen of the remainder he put into the discarded class—men repudiated by their States at the recent primaries or conventions. About fifteen were grouped in the third class as representatives of States that could not be expected to give Republican majorities in the coming election. He mentioned by name and held up to contempt and scorn

Mr. Barnes of New York, Mr. Crane of Massachusetts, Mr. Penrose of Pennsylvania, Mr. Murphy of New Jersey, Mr. Stevenson of Colorado and Mr. Guggenheim of the same State. He also referred by words of description to Mr. Calhoun of California and Mr. Lorimer of Chicago.

He compared political crimes, such as he charged against his opponents, with the crimes for which men are imprisoned, to the advantage of the latter, and declared that some of the governors among the reactionaries have refused pardons to criminals whose deeds were infinitely less wicked than the political misdemeanors of the governors themselves.

After arraigning the whole crowd of reactionaries as members of a conspiracy formed for wrecking the party, a conspiracy which the members were bent on carrying out without conscience or scruple, he announced his plan of campaign for the control of the convention. He demanded that the seventy-six delegates, whose seats are to be contested before the Credentials Committee, stand aside and allow their cases to be decided by the 1,000 uncontested delegates. He declared that it would be a fraud upon the party to allow them to take part in the convention, and that their participation would so vitiate any action of the convention which depended upon their votes that it would not be binding upon any Republican inside the Convention or outside.

This statement called forth the most spontaneous demonstration of the evening. It was apparently the statement for which they were waiting. It is evident that the Roosevelt leaders will object to contested delegates voting in the temporary chairmanship fight. What this may lead to no one can say, but only one construction can be placed upon Mr. Roosevelt's language, namely, that the progressives will not regard themselves as under any obligation to support the ticket if seventy-six contested delegates are seated and, as a result of their participation in the convention, Mr. Taft is nominated. The prospect is bright for a lively convention.

After disposing of the President, Senator Root and the National Committee, Mr. Roosevelt proceeded to make a plea for progressive Republicanism. He did not refer to any issue, but dealt with the broad distinction between the people and those who exploit them. He quoted Lincoln and interpreted his definition and distinction in the language of to-day. He described his opponents in the present contest as men of restricted vision and contracted sympathy; men who lack intensity of conviction and care only for the pleasure of the day; men who distrust the people, who are filled with an angry terror whenever there is an appeal to popular conscience and popular intelligence. They live on a low plane, and in an atmosphere in which impostors flourish.

His own associates, on the other hand, are men of faith and vision; men in whom love of righteousness burns like a flaming fire; men who spurn lives of selfishness, of slothful indulgence, etc.

It is a strong contrast that he draws. He carried me back to the day when I first learned of this world-wide, never-ending contest between the beneficiaries of privilege and the unorganized masses, and I can appreciate the amazement which he must feel that so many honest and well-meaning people seem blind or indifferent to what is going on.

I passed through the same period of amazement when I first began to run for President. My only regret is that we have not had the benefit of his powerful assistance during the campaigns in which we have protested against the domination of politics by predatory corporations. He probably feels more strongly stirred to action to-day because he was so long unconscious of the forces at work thwarting the popular will. The fact, too, that he has won prestige and position for himself and friends through the support of the very influences which he now so righteously denounces must still further increase the sense of responsibility which he feels this time.

He errs, however, and a very natural error it is, in assuming that the defeat of the progressive Republicans in this convention would be fatal to the country. He forgets that the Democrats stand ready to rescue the nation, even if the progressive Republicans fail, and then there are future campaigns if the reactionaries win this one.

He ought to find encouragement in my experience. I have seen several campaigns end in a most provoking way, and yet I have lived to see a Republican ex-president cheered by a Republican audience for denouncing men who, only a few years ago, were thought to be the custodians of the nation's honor.

This contest is an important one, and veteran reformers rejoice at the advanced ground taken by progressive Republicans, but this country is not going to ruin. A convention may delay reforms for a short time, but it cannot stay the onward march of the people. Democracy is militant the world around, and nowhere more so than in our own beloved land.

V

HOW ELIHU ROOT WAS CHOSEN TEMPORARY CHAIRMAN

Mr. Bryan's letter in morning newspapers of Wednesday, June 19th.

Chicago, June 18.—I am enjoying my position among the newspaper boys, but being a little new at this kind of work I have to confess to the commission of two blunders so far. First, I overestimated the acquaintance of the reading public here with the Bible. In my letter of this morning I referred to the ninth verse of the twentieth chapter of Matthew, supposing the Republicans attending the convention were as familiar with the text as are the Democrats, but I find they laid the reference away until they had time to look it up. Possibly it will make a deeper impression upon them when they find the verse referred to is as follows: "And when they came that were hired about the eleventh hour, they received every man a penny."

If the reader could have noted the similarity between Mr. Roosevelt's presentation of the issues between plutocracy and democracy and the speeches which have been made for nearly two decades by progressive Democrats and the speeches which have been made more recently by Senator La Follette and other pioneers among the progressive Republicans, he would have seen the aptness of the Bible quotation.

My second mistake was in not associating with

AT THE REPUBLICAN CONVENTION—MR. BRYAN ENJOYING THE DISCUSSION.
(*McCutcheon in "Collier's Weekly"—Reproduced by Permission.*)

me a sporting editor, who could give me the technical phrases of the prize ring; my vocabulary is hardly adequate for a description of the first round of the great contest which is being fought out at the Coliseum.

A little after the appointed hour of noon Victor Rosewater, of Nebraska, acting chairman of the Republican National Committee, called the convention to order and directed the secretary to read the call. As soon as the reading was completed, and before Mr. Rosewater could announce the committee's choice for temporary chairman, Gov. Hadley, of Missouri, obtained recognition and moved to substitute the names of about eighty Roosevelt contesting delegates for the Taft delegates whose names had been put upon the temporary roll-call by the committee.

This move on the part of the Progressives was evidently anticipated, for former Congressman Watson, of Indiana, was on his feet in an instant with a point of order. Chairman Rosewater said he would hold the point of order well taken, but would give both sides an opportunity to present the matter to the convention.

Mr. Hadley made the principal argument, citing three precedents—the convention of 1864, when the temporary roll-call was amended; 1880, when the temporary roll-call was again amended; and 1884, when the convention adopted the policy of considering the committee's recommendation for temporary chairman as merely suggestive and not conclusive upon the convention.

Mr. Watson replied there was no national committee in 1864 to prepare the temporary roll-call, that in 1880 the temporary chairman had already been elected before the motion to amend the temporary roll was entertained, and that in 1884 the amendment of the recommendation made by the committee as to temporary chairman was not a precedent for the case now before this convention, because in the selection of a chairman the matter was submitted to the delegates on the temporary roll, while in the present case there is no body authorized to vote on the temporary chairmanship until the temporary roll-call has been made up.

A number of speeches were made on both sides, most of them discussing the merits of the case rather than the precedents, and some of them revealing the tension under which the leaders are acting. The question was settled by the refusal of Chairman Rosewater to entertain an appeal, which left the Taft forces in control of enough votes to secure for them the temporary chairmanship.

The fight, however, was interesting enough to make the spectators feel that they were getting their money's worth. A national convention is well worth attending, especially when one can look on without being so deeply concerned in the result as to make him blind to the amusing side of the picture.

A convention is made up of partisans, who are there to help each his side, and onlookers who applaud things cleverly done, as the occupants of the grand stand cheer a baseball player when he makes a good hit. Then there is the witty man, who says something that catches the audience. They were all in evidence to-day.

The partisans were giving enthusiastic support to their representatives, and cheering the points made. Groans were not infrequent, the most spontaneous and widespread greeting Mr. Root's opening sentence when he thanked the convention for the confidence expressed in him. This interruption lasted some time and plainly embarrassed the speaker.

Another timely suggestion from the audience started a cheer when Congressman Payne was arguing "for an orderly method of procedure," meaning that the work of the steam roller should not be interfered with. Some one called out, "Tell us about the Payne-Aldrich bill." The suggestion wakened the echoes in memory's hall and those well informed recalled a number of prominent Republicans who were dragged into involuntary retirement by that same Payne-Aldrich bill, and they also remembered that it has made Mr. Taft round-shouldered to carry his part of the burden which that bill imposed upon the country.

Senator Bradley, of Kentucky, also was hectored by the audience. He had not proceeded far with his argument when some one in the audience referred to his vote in the Lorimer case. He probably was the most extreme representative of the reactionary type who appeared before the convention, and he did not shrink from defending Lorimer. He seemed ready for a fight on any phase of the contest between the progressives and the reactionaries. Mr. Heney, of California, was the most militant of the progressive speakers, and he, like Senator Bradley, spent a part of his time pausing for order to be restored.

It is interesting to compare the reasons given by the various speakers with the reasons which actually controlled them. Upon the surface of the discussion it would seem the progressives were bent on securing a fair hearing on the contested cases before either side was allowed to profit by the presence of the delegates. The reactionaries, on the other hand, seemed specially concerned in averting chaos. They could see nothing but confusion if any departure was made from the regular procedure. This was the issue presented in the speeches.

A great deal of time could have been saved if each side had explained, as each side could have explained in a word, that the eighty contested delegates held the balance of power and might decide all the important questions to come before the convention. It is not certain that the opposite side would not have exchanged arguments had the positions been changed.

All of which goes to show that a national convention is not the best place in the world to decide questions of abstract justice. The temptation to gain an unfair advantage is so great that it is not always resisted. The most effective restraint is the fear that palpable injustice may react upon the successful party at the polls, and this fear is reduced to a minimum when the fight reaches a point where neither side expects the other to win at the polls and is not sure about its own success.

The fight over the chairmanship revealed a little piece of strategy which came as a surprise to most of the audience. Mr. Root had for some weeks been known to be the choice of the Taft forces for temporary chairman, but it was generally understood that Senator Borah would be the Roosevelt candidate. Some time in the night, however, arrangements were made with the Roosevelt leaders for the presentation of the name of Gov. McGovern, of Wisconsin, by a minority of the Wisconsin delegation. This was done over the protest of Mr. La Follette and his representatives. As late as 11 o'clock in the morning the Wisconsin delegation, by a vote of 14 to 11, decided not to present a candidate for temporary chairman.

The governor's name was presented, however, by Delegate Cochems, and Wisconsin's executive received thirteen of the Wisconsin vote (just one half) and nine of the North Dakota La Follette delegates, besides the Roosevelt strength. Mr. Houser, Senator La Follette's spokesman, stated the facts in order that the senator might not be accused of tying up with either side. Mr. Houser and several other members of the Wisconsin delegates voted for Mr. Lauder, of North Dakota.

Senator Root received 558 votes, eighteen more than half the convention, but as a number of Mr. Root's votes came from men who are instructed for Mr. Roosevelt, the presidential situation is still in doubt.

I would want to make three guesses if I were compelled to guess at all. First, that Mr. Taft may be nominated as the result of the putting of the names of the Taft contestants on the temporary roll. This gives the Taft men control of the committee on credentials, and the Taft contestants can be seated if they are allowed to vote for themselves. Second, Mr. Roosevelt may be nominated if he can get some of his contestants seated, or can make inroads upon the southern delegates. Third, Mr. La Follette and Mr. Cummins may hold the balance of power and compel the nomination of a third candidate, name unknown. Thus endeth the first day of the convention.

VI

AN ANALYSIS OF THE CHAIRMANSHIP CONTEST

Mr. Bryan's letter in afternoon newspapers of Wednesday, June 19th.

Chicago, June 19.—The first day's round of the wrestling match in which the Republican leaders are engaging resulted in a dogfall. Mr. Root received 558 votes for temporary chairman—only eighteen more than half of the convention—which indicates that the vote between Mr. Taft and Mr. Roosevelt will be so close that no one can count with any certainty on the result.

On the face of the returns it would look like a victory for Taft. It is a great advantage to him to have a supporter in the chair, especially as able a man as Mr. Root. He is probably the most skilful corporation lawyer in the country. One of his prominent clients has been quoted as saying that former attorneys employed by him told him what he could not do, but that Root told him how he could do things. The New York senator will be in a position where he can do things, and from now on the Roosevelt forces can expect no parliamentary advantage. It will keep them busy to avoid the traps and pitfalls that will be set for them. In fact, it would not be surprising if our old friend, Res Adjudicata, appeared on the scene every now and then when least expected.

But while Mr. Taft has won the temporary chairmanship, his victory belongs to that class of victories of which it can be said that a few more such would destroy the victor. In order to win the coveted prize Mr. Root had to secure seven of Mr. Roosevelt's instructed delegates in Maryland, three in Oregon and four in Pennsylvania. These men are under instructions given at primaries and will have to vote for Roosevelt on roll-call. These twenty-two reduce the Taft strength below the 540 necessary for his nomination, and there are a number of other Roosevelt delegates pledged, but not instructed, who voted for Mr. Root. It will be seen, therefore, that Mr. Taft is still some distance from the nomination, even if all of his contested delegates are seated. It is barely possible, though not probable, that some of Mr. Taft's uninstructed delegates may revolt against the seating of some of the contested delegates, and then allowance must be made for inroads on the susceptible portion of Mr. Taft's following.

Mr. Taft's managers, however, are presenting a

bold front and are claiming 100 Roosevelt delegates on the second ballot. The ex-President doubtless feels some chagrin at the result of the fight on the temporary chairmanship, but Senator Dixon uses the vote cast for Mr. Root as proof that Mr. Taft is whipped. This does not, however, mean that Mr. Roosevelt will be nominated. It is easier to prevent Mr. Taft's nomination than to secure his own. Senator La Follette's thirty-six votes and Senator Cummins's ten votes will contribute to the defeat of Mr. Taft, but they will not be of much service to Mr. Roosevelt; at least they have not been counted in the Roosevelt column. The alliance formed yesterday between the Roosevelt following and a minority of the Wisconsin delegation may indicate a willingness of some of the La Follette men to switch to Roosevelt if La Follette retires from the race.

Nine of the ten North Dakota delegates joined the Roosevelt delegates in supporting McGovern, and the ten Cummins men from Iowa also voted for McGovern. While this does not commit them to Roosevelt it indicates a willingness to side with the followers of the ex-President rather than with the followers of the President when they are compelled to choose.

The pot has been boiling furiously since the first session adjourned, and one hears all sorts of rumors. While it is not safe to venture a prediction, still it is only reflecting what one hears in the corridors to say that there is more talk of a dark horse than heretofore. The two principal contestants have measured strength and neither feels as sure as he did before the roll-call.

The office-seeker is not idle, and the paramount question with him is not who would make an ideal candidate, or an ideal president, but who can win. Mr. Taft and Mr. Roosevelt will find some consolation in killing each other off, and both may prefer to support a third man rather than risk the support of one by the other.

Cummins and Borah are the persons talked of most as compromise candidates. It ought to be easy for the Roosevelt men to support Borah, and the Taft men would probably find it easier to support Cummins than any other progressive.

The reader may think the above review of the situation somewhat indefinite—if so, he is in the attitude of mind that best befits one who has surveyed the field as it appears to-day. It is any man's race at this time.

The convention yesterday was full of interesting incidents, and no one has complained that the performance was not up to the promises made in advance. Even a Democrat must admit that the delegates are a fine looking body of men; they are the pick of the Republican party of the nation. There are a number of prominent Republicans who did not secure commissions as delegates, but most of them are here in an advisory capacity. It is interesting to note how the sifting process eliminates the relatively inferior and brings before the footlights the men who are intellectually prepared for the contest.

Gov. Hadley, of Missouri, led the fight against the temporary roll of delegates, and he made a splendid impression. His argument was clear and well presented. His manner was pleasing and he held the attention of the audience.

Watson, of Indiana, justified the confidence reposed in him by the Taft leaders. His speech was well put together, and his argumentative manner was suited to the work he had in hand. Job Hedges, of New York, acquitted himself most creditably. His special task was to inform the audience of Mr. Roosevelt's high opinion of Mr. Root, and he performed it with dramatic art.

Then there were speakers who did not catch the spirit of the occasion; at least not in time to save themselves from the hasty judgment which a convention audience stands ready to pronounce. This judgment is not always accurate, but it is not usually subject to reversal. When a convention crowd turns against a speaker the sooner he brings his remarks to a close the better. A great deal depends on getting off on the right foot. An explanation or an apology is sometimes fatal. The tone of voice or an awkward gesture may call down the derision of the audience, and then it is all over.

One of the most humorous incidents in convention history occurred at Chicago sixteen years ago. A Louisiana delegate paused in the course of his speech to take a swallow of water. Some interruption prevented his resumption at once, and he picked up the glass a second and a third time. Then some one in the audience suggested that he take another drink, and from that time on he was on the water wagon. Pages brought him buckets of water, and the audience was convulsed for a quarter of an hour. One man in yesterday's convention began in a manner that aroused the religious fervor of one delegate to the extent of calling forth an amen, while another speaker put his arms in a position that made some of the delegates discuss aviation.

The people who gather at a convention, however, are good humored, and while they are sometimes unmanageable, they are not malicious. The only way one can get even is to enjoy the turn of fortune that brings others, for the time being, into the position of making fun for the audience.

A convention is a splendid place to study human nature; man in a crowd is quite a different creature from man acting alone. Enthusiasm is contagious, although in this convention the friends of the two leading candidates have thus far been able to restrain themselves from joining in each others' demonstrations, except when a wave of laughter sweeps the hall. We are having a great time.

VII

THE ROOSEVELT-HADLEY DEMONSTRATION

Mr. Bryan's letter in morning newspapers of Thursday, June 20th.

Chicago, June 19.—Wednesday's session of the convention surpassed Tuesday's in interest, and I shall deal with the most spectacular feature of it first, viz., the demonstration. We had nothing Tuesday that rose to the dignity of a demonstration, at least nothing that compared with the outburst of yesterday, and it may be worth while to devote a few sentences to this peculiar and fascinating phase of convention activities. A demonstration is a hard thing to manufacture, but an easy thing to enlarge. There must be spontaneity about it to make it a genuine success, but given the element of unpreparedness as a basis any amount of prepared material can be profitably used.

The day's session was interrupted for about forty-five minutes, more or less, and during that time the usual number of eccentric persons and unique features appeared for the entertainment of the convention's guests. Powder is a harmless thing so long as its serenity is not disturbed by some obtrusive spark, but when the spark comes into contact with the powder the powder, as a matter of self-respect, must resent the insult and resent it instantly. There was powder in abundance, and the spark, much to its own surprise, got too near the powder, and then all was off for a while.

Ex-Congressman Watson, of Indiana, was presenting the Taft cause and was doing it acceptably to his side of the house. In fact, he was making a plausible argument. To clinch it he said that even Gov. Hadley had expressed a willingness to refer the contests to the credentials committee under certain conditions and with certain qualifications.

This statement at once raised in the minds of those who listened a question as to what the conditions and qualifications were. The interest at once became intense, for any surrender or compromise on Gov. Hadley's part would have been a victory for Mr. Taft's followers, while any misrepresentation on the part of Mr. Watson would demand immediate contradiction.

Gov. Hadley was quick to size up the situation, and when Mr. Watson turned to him for some sign of confirmation he arose and stepped to the speakers' stand. The audience rose at once in anticipation of a conflict in statement and the suppressed feeling burst forth. It was a Roosevelt demonstration and was the most significant expression that the audience has thus far given of sympathy with the ex-President, or at least opposition to the President.

After there had been enough cheering to get the Roosevelt delegates well warmed up the delegations began to move about the hall. Some of the standards were carried in a parade through the aisles, with delegates young and old marching with lock step. The audience was on its feet, a considerable portion joining in the shouting as best it could. The Roosevelt leaders were all in evidence. Gov. Stubbs, occupying a position to one side of the delegate space, stood upon a chair and waved his handkerchief with an enthusiasm that a younger man could hardly have exhibited.

While the tumult was at its height attention was attracted to a woman in white, who stood in the front row of the gallery and waved a picture of Mr. Roosevelt. She was soon the center of attraction, and the more enthusiastic of the Roosevelt delegates flocked to that side of the hall. Soon a California bear, a golden figure that indicates the California section of the hall, was seen swaying back and forth near the lady with the picture. After a few minutes of gesticulation she was escorted down from the gallery and up to the speakers' stand, where she led the applause for a while. Finally the shouting and the tumult ceased and the audience, exhausted by its efforts, subsided and quiet was restored. It is only fair to the Taft delegates to say that they preserved a proper decorum during the entire performance, their faces wearing an expression suited to the occasion.

While the demonstration lasted there was a good deal of discussion as to the meaning of it, and people asked each other, "Is this a Roosevelt stampede?" "Is this a boom for Hadley, as a compromise candidate?" etc. And what did it mean? The result of the vote which followed showed that there was no break in the Taft battle line—on the contrary, he went out of the convention stronger than on Tuesday. It helped Hadley. There is no doubt that Gov. Hadley has made friends every time he has appeared. His personality pleases and his manner is conciliating. It is only fair to add him to the list of compromise candidates now under consideration, although the second victory for Mr. Taft naturally decreases the talk of a compromise.

The demonstration was not so important an hour after it was over as it seemed when at its height. It illustrates how much noise can be turned loose in a convention without materially affecting the result. Stampedes are about as much exaggerated in effect as what is known as personal popularity is in quantity. Nothing is more likely to be overestimated in politics than that peculiar quality known as personal popularity.

While every one who lives as he should can count upon personal friends who will be attached to him regardless of his political views, still the substantial strength of a public man is due to the things he stands for. In politics men are measured by the service they can render—a fact which can be verified by even a casual reading of history.

Popular idols fall when they turn from a principle or policy to which their friends are wedded. And, so, people magnify the influence exerted upon a convention by a demonstration. Many stampedes are attempted, but few succeed, and those that do succeed owe their success to some material fact upon which the demonstration merely turns the light.

The delegates who attend a national convention are generally there for a purpose, and they are not easily swerved from it. A convention feels about demonstrations, such as occurred yesterday, somewhat like the big man felt who had a small wife who was in the habit of whipping him. When asked why he permitted it, he replied that it seemed to please her and did not hurt him.

But a word in regard to the merits of the discussion. As on Tuesday the speeches were able and gave an opportunity for the audience to take the measure of a number of men. Allen, of Kansas, made a favorable impression, as did Morrison, of

Arizona; Hemenway, of Indiana; Devine, of Colorado, and Littleton, of Texas. Gov. Deneen, of Illinois, received an ovation when he appeared with his amendment to Gov. Hadley's motion. And, speaking of favorable impressions, John M. Harlan, Jr., won the audience with his voice. If there is anything that a convention loves it is a voice that can be heard. Harlan is richly endowed in this respect, so richly that a megaphone diminishes rather than increases the effectiveness of his voice.

Probably no man has made more capital out of his appearance than George L. Record, of New Jersey, did. He approached the subject in a judicial way, and presented his argument with such an appearance of fairness that he captivated the audience, or would have done so if it had been open to captivation.

But convention audiences are not like juries, made up of those who are unprejudiced, nor like popular audiences, made up of people who act only for themselves and therefore are free to follow their inclinations.

And this brings me to the point in the case. Those unfamiliar with conventions doubtless wondered why the arguments advanced made no change in the vote. That is easily explained. The delegates are sent there largely under instructions, expressed or implied, and they are there to do anything within reason—and reason's limitations are somewhat elastic—to accomplish their purpose. Every delegate knew what the speakers seemed to overlook—namely: that the seating of the seventy-odd contesting delegates would in all probability decide the convention's actions. The Taft men had charge of the national committee. By seating the Taft delegates they were able to give Mr. Taft's friends a majority on the temporary roll-call. This majority could organize the convention and give Mr. Taft's friends the temporary chairman.

As the credentials committee is made up from the delegates appearing on the temporary roll-call, this would give the Taft men a majority of the credentials committee, and secure them a majority report. The delegates on the temporary roll-call would then approve the report and seat the Taft contestants. Everything, therefore, depended on not allowing any break in the program.

The Roosevelt men, on the other hand, knew that if they could seat their own contesting delegates before proceeding with the election of temporary chairman or even compel Mr. Taft's contesting delegates to refrain from voting they could secure the temporary organization, a majority of the credentials committee, a favorable report from the committee, and the approval of the report by the convention.

The arguments made by the Taft men had in

view the securing of a Taft convention; the arguments made by the Roosevelt men had in view the securing of a Roosevelt convention, and each side knew what the other side was after.

If the Roosevelt men had had control of the national committee there is no doubt that they would have seated their men, and it is quite probable that they would not have been looking for precedents to sustain the position which they are taking.

But, the reader will ask, is there no standard of right and wrong that a convention is bound to respect? Is all this talk about justice, honesty, and a square deal buncombe? No. People want to be honest, but they are apt to be unconsciously biased. It is fear of this unconscious bias that leads us to enact laws forbidding a judge to try his own case or a juror to serve in a case in which he has any interest. We recognize that no man is good enough to decide an important disputed matter in which he has a substantial personal interest. And it is no reflection on the high character of our citizens.

Neither is it a reflection upon the bench of our country to say that our judges are apt to be influenced by political bias in deciding political questions. It is not strange, therefore, that the delegates in this Republican convention should have divided upon this vital question according to their choice for president.

I lay no claim to freedom from bias, but I believe that the position taken by the Roosevelt men makes a nearer approach to justice than the position taken by the Taft men. First, because the delegates to the convention have been chosen since the national committee was chosen. The national committee was selected four years ago, while the delegates are fresh from the people; the delegates, therefore, are more likely to represent the voters than the old committee. In the second place, the delegates are more numerous, and it would be more difficult to lead the same proportion of them to do an act of injustice; and, third, the delegates go back to their people, like a discharged jury, and are therefore more amenable to public sentiment.

But whatever change is made in the rules must usually be made for conventions in advance; impartiality cannot be expected where great feeling exists. The prayer, "Lead us not into temptation," is full of meaning.

VIII

THE FUTILITY OF THE DEMONSTRATION

Mr. Bryan's letter in afternoon newspapers of Thursday, June 20th.

Chicago, June 20.—"Button, button, who has the button?" The question is suggested by the uncertainty that prevails here. There are three uncertainties to be considered in this report. First, what did the demonstration mean? Why did the convention leap to its feet in an instant, shout itself hoarse, work itself into weariness, and then subside exhausted? In describing the convention as having held a demonstration, reference is made, of course, only to those who participated, and not all participated. The Taft delegates looked upon it with ill-disguised disfavor. It was interesting to note the difference in the expression upon their faces and the smiling countenances of the Roosevelt men.

A few of the Taft men manifested an interest in the beginning, when some took advantage of the enthusiasm to work up a Hadley boom. Some of the New York delegation wickedly harbored the thought that they could excite rivalry between the governor of Missouri* and the ex-president. They seemed to think that a little jealousy would not be out of harmony with "the orderly proceedings" which they so staunchly contend for. Gov. Hadley started it, or rather Watson started it, by calling Hadley to the front. It was the psychological moment. What happened could not have been arranged for by any national committee, and the tumult could not have been smoothed out by a steam roller until the pent-up feeling had a chance to escape.

When in a controversy one man makes a positive statement, and the other replies that the gentleman has told what he knows to be untrue, the bystanders generally prick up their ears in expectation. So it was at the convention. Mr. Watson, of Indiana, in the course of a persuasive speech, sought to add weight to his appeal by saying that Gov. Hadley had expressed himself as willing to leave the whole matter to the credentials committee, with certain qualifications and conditions. As Gov. Hadley had made the motion to remove the contested Taft delegates from the temporary roll, this was virtually a charge that the governor had agreed to a compromise.

The Roosevelt men were not in a compromising mood, and they at once questioned the correctness

* Hadley.

of Mr. Watson's statement. Mr. Watson turned to Gov. Hadley for confirmation, and Gov. Hadley, who immediately rose to reply, came forward in a way that announced in advance a contradiction of Mr. Watson's statement. At least that was what the audience saw in his manner, and the demonstration began. It lasted about forty-five minutes, during which time old and young, men and women, participated to the limit of their strength.

It is interesting to watch a crowd when people are swept along by a wave of enthusiasm. There are certain things to be expected in a convention demonstration. People stand on chairs when they cannot find anything higher; they wave their handkerchiefs and shout. They march around the hall in procession, carrying flags and banners. Anything that will add to the noise is likely to be called into use.

When the delegates begin to carry standards heroes begin to develop. The first man to grab the standard becomes the leader, and he tells his grandchildren how he took it away from a man bigger than himself. Then there is the fellow who will not let the delegation have the standard. The Illinois standard was guarded against all comers by a man whose friends will doubtless present his name for a Carnegie medal.

Some of the women will be tired and worn to-day as the result of their part in the great spectacle.

One lady occupied the center of the stage for ten or fifteen minutes, first in the gallery, where she appeared dressed in white, vigorously waving a picture of Mr. Roosevelt and shouting words of praise. It was not long before some of the delegates made their way to the gallery and escorted her to the speakers' stand, where she led the cheering. Then a procession was formed, which she conducted through the aisles. At last she found her way back to the place whence she started, and was about to renew her efforts when the police interfered.

It was interesting to note that one of the conspicuous sections of the gallery reserved for a striking array of women supporters of President Taft attracted attention at this time. The ladies had been quite demonstrative when the Taft speakers made a hit, but they refrained from applause when the audience was in eruption over the Watson-Hadley incident. They cheered vigorously, however, when the police quelled the lady in white.

Now that the demonstration is over—and what would a convention be without a demonstration?—the convention can proceed with its work. The Roosevelt enthusiasm has had its vent, Gov. Hadley has had his ovation, and the Taft delegates have had their chance to laugh over the futility of the attempt at a stampede. All are happy and the spectators have seen the sight that, more than anything else, makes a convention worth attending to the average spectator.

But what of the issue that has brought forth so much discussion? What of the "larceny of delegates," the "theft of States," and "the outrageous injustice" on the one side, and the demand for "fair play," "even-handed equity" and a "square deal" on the other? Must "right be forever on the scaffold and wrong forever on the throne?" You would think so to see the machine at work in spite of all that is said in protest. It is all an interesting study, especially to one who can watch it without feeling that any of his near relatives are in jeopardy.

One amusing thing about it all is the lack of frankness in the speeches. Each side gives reasons that do not influence the men who give them. Mr. Taft has control of the national committee, and the national committee seated the Taft delegates. Did not the national committee act in the same way four years ago when the friends of Mr. Fairbanks, Mr. Cannon and Mr. Hughes were complaining of the Roosevelt steam roller? And does any one doubt that the committee would have put on the Roosevelt delegates and kept them there if Mr. Roosevelt's friends had had control? If the Roosevelt men were in control of the committee and needed the contested delegates to make up a majority would they not have felt that the end justified the means, especially if that was the only way that "the bosses could be dethroned" and the rank and file of the Republican party put in a position to dictate the nomination? I would not attempt to answer the question, but the old story that we learn in the blue-backed speller about the ownership of the ox that was bored comes quite naturally to one's mind on such an occasion.

One cannot be but impressed with the intention of the delegates in both of these contending groups. There are not many men in the convention who are actually bent on ruining the country. The men on both sides think they are serving their party and their country both. It is a matter of bias; they look at questions from a different standpoint. The Taft men think the progressives are dangerously radical and the Roosevelt men think the stand-patters are dangerously conservative.

Both of these forces are needed in every country. If it were not for the conservatives the radicals would go too fast; if it were not for the radicals the conservatives would not go at all. Progress lies between the two extremes and good will come out of this convention, no matter how it terminates.

National conventions are great educational institutions, whether those who get them up intend it or not. I began attending national conventions when I was sixteen years old. I have attended six Democratic national conventions and am on my way to the seventh. I have in fact attended every Democratic national convention except the convention of 1880, since 1876 (omitting, of course, the conventions of 1900 and 1908, when I was a candidate). This is my second Republican convention, the first being the convention of 1896, when a part of the Republican convention walked out as a protest against the platform.

There is not likely to be any serious controversy over the platform this year, at least one hears no talk of platforms among the delegates. The element that controls the convention will control the platform. If the Taft men control the convention they will try to make a platform that will please as many progressives as possible; if, on the other hand, the progressives get control of the convention they will be interested in writing a platform which will hold as many conservatives as possible.

When the emphasis is placed upon the candidate, as here, the platform is likely to be used to aid the candidates, as far as it can be done without the absolute surrender of principle. And who is the candidate to-day? Echo answers: Who?

The Taft men feel more confident than they did yesterday morning, and yet there is persistent talk of a compromise ticket. Hughes and Hadley form one combination; it is alliterative and it would surely be all-comprehending. Justice Hughes ought to suit the reactionaries, and Gov. Hadley is popular with the progressives, but can they get together on such a ticket, or on any ticket?

IX

ON THE EVE OF THE CRISIS IN THE CONVENTION

Mr. Bryan's letter in the morning newspapers of Friday, June 21st.

Chicago, June 20.—Dickens, in his Mudfog papers, has a correspondent sending a bulletin to his paper to announce that nothing had happened since his last bulletin, dispatched fifteen minutes earlier. This letter will be somewhat of the same character.

The third session of the convention was called to order at 11 o'clock to-day, and an immediate recess was taken until 4. At 4 the convention was called to order and adjourned until 11 Friday. This left Thursday without convention incidents—a lull between the demonstration of the day before and the storm which seems brewing for to-morrow.

The credentials committee is engaged in considering the contests, and from the progress that is being made it seems likely that it will take a good while to get through. The first meeting of the committee was marked by outbursts of passion which threatened the disruption of the party. In fact, the Roosevelt portion of the committee withdrew twice, declaring that they would organize a separate convention.

The majority of the members are Taft men and they started in to make short work of the contests. They proposed to allow five minutes each to district contestants and ten minutes where the contestant was a delegate at large, the cases to be submitted without argument. This was so objectionable to the minority that the Roosevelt members refused to go any further. After consultation with the Roosevelt leaders the minority returned to the committee room, but were soon rebellious and quit a second time.

Various rumors were afloat in the morning as to what the Roosevelt men intended to do. Various estimates were placed upon the number of those who were willing to burn the bridges behind them and embark upon a new party movement, or perhaps it should not be called a new party, for the proposed bolt is intended as a means of obtaining control of the Republican party.

These conflicting statements continued until late in the afternoon, when the ex-president gave out a statement that set all doubts at rest. He declared that he is willing to accept a nomination either as the candidate of the "honestly elected majority," meaning a convention made up of the Roosevelt delegates now on the temporary roll-call with the

Roosevelt contestants substituted for the Taft delegates whose title is contested, or, to cover all possible contingencies, he is willing to accept a nomination from any part of the progressive element that is willing to bolt.

To use his own language, he says, "if some among them fear to take such a stand, and the remainder choose to inaugurate a movement to nominate me for the presidency as a progressive on a progressive platform, and if in such an event the general feeling among the progressives favors my being nominated, I shall accept." He adds: "In either case I shall make an appeal to every honest citizen in the nation; and I shall fight the campaign through, win or lose, even if I do not get a single electoral vote."

This statement breathes the spirit of a fighter and arouses the enthusiasm of the more radical of the followers of Mr. Roosevelt. The only loophole in the statement is the phrase, "and if, in such event, the general feeling among progressives favors my being nominated." That would indicate an intention to take a little time after the convention to ascertain the "general feeling." And the "general feeling among progressives" may depend largely upon the action of the regular convention after the bolters leave.

Mr. Roosevelt generously releases such progressives as do not choose to follow him. His statement recalls a dramatic act in the career of Pizarro when his followers mutinied after a series of reverses. The Spanish conqueror made a speech to them, recounting the hardships through which they had passed, and pointed out the dangers which were before them. Then, drawing a line on the sand with his sword, he invited those to follow him who were not afraid to die.

The story need not be carried farther. The crisis of the convention is at hand. The stand-patters regard his statement as a bluff and many of them would be glad to see him carry out the course he has outlined. They want him to bolt. They have confidence in their ability to drive him into retirement. They have certainly given him every provocation; there has not been a suggestion of compromise since the fight began. They have carried out their program to the letter, and the steam roller, as their machine is called, moves on with regularity and precision. They even have chains on the wheels to prevent skidding.

It is no pleasant situation in which the ex-president finds himself, nor is it an ordinary situation. Twice chief executive of the nation, the second time elected by the largest majority that a president ever received; the recipient of honors in foreign lands and supreme dictator in his own party, he now finds the man whom he nominated and elected pitted against him in the most bitter contest that our country has ever seen, and he sees that opponent operating with the skill of a past master the very machinery which the tutor constructed and taught him to use. And then the ex-president after failing—as he seems to have failed—to control the convention announces his willingness to bolt and lead a forlorn hope, the only probable effect of which will be the defeat of both and the election of a Democratic president! Surely the ways of Providence are mysterious!

There is still a way of escape, however, for the present and past occupants of the White House. They can withdraw and allow a third man to be chosen. This would seem to be the thing most likely at present. Mr. Roosevelt has apparently lost out, but he has the power to make the victory of his opponent a barren one. Mr. Taft has received a "vindication," the value of which will depend upon the opinion people have of the character of his supporters and of the methods employed by them. Does Mr. Taft want to convert his convention vindication into a defeat at the polls? Or will he content himself with the consoling thought that by retiring he sacrifices his own ambition to his party's welfare. I do not like to conclude this report with a series of questions, but question marks loom large in Chicago at this time.

X

THE CONVENTION AS A PHOTOGRAPH OF THE NATION

Mr. Bryan's letter in afternoon newspapers of Friday, June 21st.

Chicago, June 21.—While we are waiting for the situation to clear up let us consider a phase of this convention which should not escape notice, namely, the evidence that it gives of the capacity of the American people for self-government.

Individuals differ in the amount of self-restraint they exercise, and self-restraint is quite an accurate measure of capacity for self-government. The individual who permits his body to have free rein soon destroys himself. The mind must subjugate the body and keep it under control before a human being is worthy to be called a man. But mental control is not sufficient. The mind may control the body, but the mind itself may run wild. Without a moral balance wheel a brilliant mind may use both itself and the body for great harm.

Solomon tells us "that he that ruleth his own spirit is greater than he that taketh a city."

Where there is the highest average of intellectual and moral power, with the moral in control, there is the highest average of citizenship. Our nation is making progress because it has a high average of citizenship—a larger percentage of its people than in any other country have the intelligence to estimate the problems with which they have to deal and the moral strength to grapple with those problems.

This convention is, in a way, a photograph of the nation. All the great forces that exert a potential influence in our country are here in person or by proxy. Democracy has its champions, aristocracy has its representatives, and plutocracy its agents. The poor are not without spokesmen; neither is accumulated wealth without its advocates.

The convention hall is like an arena in which a gladiatorial contest is being waged. Strong men and fair women look down from the galleries while the participants in the great conflict battle over policies and principles. It is remarkable that so much intensity of speech, so much tenacity of purpose, so much depth of conviction can be brought together on opposite sides with so little display of anger and such an absence of rudeness.

The convention is nearly equally divided, the Roosevelt men believing that Mr. Taft represents organized greed, legislative pillage and political corruption carried to the seventh power, and some have expressed themselves on the subject in no uncertain terms. The Taft men, on the other hand, think that the Roosevelt crowd is largely made up of self-seeking politicians who are willing to resort to demagogic appeals to secure their ends, men who stir up the passions of the multitudes against law, order and property. This opinion has also been expressed quite freely for some months.

Now the most distinguished leaders of these two elements in the Republican party are brought face to face in one room and are permitted to speak their feelings freely to each other. States are divided by narrow aisles and these antagonists see each other at close range.

Mr. Barnes, who is not able to produce a certificate of character from Mr. Roosevelt less than a year old, rubs against Mr. Flinn, whom President Taft cannot regard with any degree of allowance, and yet there is no physical combat. The Massachusetts delegation is divided half and half; eighteen "demagogues" and a group of eighteen more, made of "bosses," "corrupt politicians" and "representatives of predatory wealth," and yet there has not been a fight. Several of the delegations are divided, some in the middle and some on the edges, but the best of decorum prevails.

Even Senator Bradley, of Kentucky, and Mr. Heney, of California, can appear upon the same platform without disturbing the peace. They have their differences and they are fighting them out, but they are doing it in a most creditable way. I am not now passing on the merits of the decisions rendered. Neither am I endorsing the parliamentary methods employed, but I congratulate the Republican party on the splendid proof it has given of the ability of a large number of people, intensely in earnest, to discuss their differences calmly, and settle the questions involved without recourse to violence. It not only indicates self-restraint, but faith in the incorruptibility of the people, the court of last resort in a republic.

This report must be put on the wires before the convention opens at 11 a. m., and it is impossible at this time to forecast the action that the convention will take. Mr. Roosevelt's statement has not changed the attitude of the Taft forces in the least. The credentials committee is entirely in the hands of the administration and the Taft delegates are being seated as rapidly as the cases can be disposed of. The contest over the length of time to be given to each case was really "much ado about nothing," because the action of the committee is sure to be the same, whether much time or little is given in each case. The facts are thoroughly understood by both sides and the hearings are merely a matter of form.

Unless something unexpected happens the Taft delegates will be seated, and it looks now as if the regular convention would renominate the President.

Some of his delegates, it is said, would prefer a compromise candidate, but the amiable gentleman in the White House is showing that he can "sit tight" when necessary. His fighting blood is aroused, and if anybody says "enough" the word is not likely to come from any one living east of the Alleghanies. At present Mr. Taft has the best of the situation and it looks as if he had made up his mind to run the ex-president out of the Republican party, or make him swallow his words.

Mr. Roosevelt is apparently facing the crisis in his political career. Bolting is easy where one is not a candidate, but it is a more difficult thing where followers are necessary. If Mr. Roosevelt could take his delegates with him he could organize a convention that would represent a majority of the Republican vote of the country, but he cannot do so.

A considerable number of his delegates will not bolt and his convention, therefore, would not carry with it the moral force that goes with the majority. He cannot tell, until the split comes, exactly how many will walk out, for some are unwilling to decide the question until the time arrives for action. If the President's followers bolt and nominate him he cannot tell whether to accept or not until after the regular convention acts, and even then he would likely be influenced by the action of the Democratic national convention.

He may be put in the attitude, therefore, of refusing to lead a bolt after he has encouraged it. If the Democrats are guilty of the criminal folly of nominating a reactionary, they will supply Mr. Roosevelt with the one thing needful in case he becomes an independent candidate, namely, an issue, and with two reactionaries running for president he might win and thus entrench himself in power. This convention, therefore, may exert a powerful influence on the Baltimore convention.

XI

CALIFORNIA'S DAY

Mr. Bryan's letter in morning newspapers of Saturday, June 22d.

Chicago, June 21.—Friday was California's day. That State occupied the center of the stage and came nearer breaking through the Taft line than any other State has done. Gov. Hadley had charge of the case for California, but he yielded to Mr. Heney to open and to Gov. Johnson to close.

Mr. Heney's speech was a strong, clear, argumentative appeal and he raised the Roosevelt followers to their feet when, after describing the President's participation in the selection of the delegates in accordance with the letter of the primary law, he charged him with treason to popular government when he attempted to repudiate the law for the sake of two delegates.

Gov. Johnson, however, was the hero of the day. His speech was, all things considered, the gem of the convention so far. He is a young man, prepossessing in appearance, full of earnestness, and his speech has the ring of sincerity. He made a plea for the progressive cause that surpassed in effectiveness anything heretofore presented to the delegates. His prophecy of victory for progressiveness this fall thrilled his hearers. He dealt with all phases of the subject, condensing what he had to say on each point into a sentence.

He told how the predatory interests had controlled his State for a generation; how at last the tide of reform had swept them out of office and given the progressives control; how the progressives, instead of using the party machinery to secure a delegation to the national convention, passed a primary law that vested control in the voters; how the reactionaries, to escape from the influence of the State organization then in the hands of the progressives, unitedly supported the primary law; how both sides selected a list of delegates in accordance with the law; how President Taft himself gave to his list of delegates the written approval required by law; how all these steps had been taken without objection and without protest; and then how these two delegates, after having been defeated by 77,000 in the State, sought to repudiate their own act and the action of the President and claim election in a district in spite of the fact that it was impossible to ascertain the exact number of votes cast in their district because fourteen precincts were partly in one district and partly in another.

He convinced the audience that he had justice on his side, but the audience was not in position to follow its convictions. A number of delegates told me that they had to vote for the two Taft delegates in order to save the Taft forces from the mortification of defeat, but that the contest ought never to have been made.

Gov. Johnson had the satisfaction of seeing the Taft majority whittled down to thirteen, and the administration will find thirteen an unlucky number out in California this fall.

It is surprising that men as intelligent as the leaders of the Taft forces would make the tactical mistake that they have in this case. In some of the contests they have made such a strong showing that even the Roosevelt members of the committee have voted with them, but one case like the California case imparts its weakness to all the others.

If it had been purely a question of principle there would have been standing ground on both sides of the issue. Gov. Johnson emphasized the right of a State to regulate its own affairs and insisted that the State law should take precedence over a rule of the national convention.

Mr. Watson, of Indiana, representing the Taft forces, laid great stress on the rules adopted by the national convention, recognizing the congressional district as the unit. There is strength in both arguments.

If I were deciding the case I would say that the State law ought to be respected but that the State made a mistake in substituting a statewide delegation for the district system.

The California case really established a unit rule by law, whereas the Republican party has come near to the people in giving each district a chance to name and instruct its delegates. It is no argument against the primary system to say that a primary law ought to recognize the district system rather than a State wide system in the selection of delegates.

While the Taft men were strong in asserting opposition to the unit rule they were weak in attempting to overthrow the primary law after they had acquiesced in it and secured the President's approval of it, and they were weak also because of their inability to show with exactness the number of votes cast in the district which they claimed to have carried by an extremely small majority.

The convention was in a good humor. The rollcall was demanded only in the case of a few States, and the delegates who were being defeated seemed to enjoy themselves about as much as those who were winning. Sometimes all the delegates would join in shouting "aye" on a viva voce vote, and then all would join in shouting "no" when the negative was put. It was impossible for Chairman Root to tell on which side the majority was, but he knew what it would be on roll-call and so declared "the ayes have it," and then the audience would break out into laughter.

The machine has worked beautifully all day; it has not slipped a cog. When it was running at full speed "Toot," "Toot," would occasionally come from the audience. Sometimes sounds arose that resembled escaping steam, but I am satisfied that no steam escaped; it was all being used, and at high pressure, too.

The platform is said to be ready, but there is little discussion of the platform. The fight has centered in men rather than in measures. Rumors have it that the Taft men, having won out on everything else, are inclined to make some concessions to progressives in the wording of the platform.

From present indications Mr. Taft will be nominated on the first ballot, or upon the second if not upon the first. The President discountenances compromise and seems prepared to stake his all upon the result. It is probable, therefore, that the platform will be to his liking and that he will have the privilege of trying the realities of an election. Nearly half of the convention will feel like concluding his nomination as a judge concludes the death sentence of a prisoner:

"And may the Lord have mercy on your soul."

XII

THE DAY BEFORE THE LAST

Mr. Bryan's letter in afternoon newspapers of Saturday, June 22d.

Chicago, Ill., June 22.—This convention seems likely to make up in quantity what it lacks as a producer of harmony. Here it is Saturday, and the committee on credentials is still at work trying to determine who are rightfully entitled to sit in a convention that assembled last Tuesday. Those who were honored by a place on the temporary roll-call are still there, and those who failed to secure recognition at the hands of the national committee are still in outer darkness, but the machine moves on.

The Taft forces lack a little more than fifty of the number of the "Light Brigade," but they seem as little dismayed as the heroic band of which we read in our school days: "Cannon to the right of them, cannon to the left of them, cannon in front of them, volleyed and thundered. Stormed at with shot and shell, boldly they rode and well, into the jaws of death, into the mouth of hell"—but I shall stop here, as I do not care to express an opinion as to the character of the combatants.

It looks, however, at this time as if the 550 were going to make their escape from the jaws of death, so far as the convention is concerned, but we shall not know until the election what fate awaits Mr. Taft's brigade.

If we can judge by what happened yesterday there has been an inexcusable waste of time. The deliberations of the committee on credentials have not resulted in throwing any new light on the subject. The reports have been stereotyped, and the convention has dealt with them without much reference to the merits of the case. I spoke of a waste of time, but the time was not really wasted. The audience had a chance to enjoy itself, several new men appeared in the moving picture that crossed the stage, and the convention entered upon an era of good feeling.

Man has been described as the animal that laughs, and but few of the delegates, if any, have failed to manifest this trait. Men who glared at each other a few days ago now chat together and joke over the situation. Man is a queer creature, and nowhere more queer than in a convention. He is like powder—more dangerous when confined than when free.

When the credentials committee attempted to rush the contests through, giving but a few minutes to each, there were angry protests and threats of a bolt. Finally the committee conceded time, as much time as the minority wanted, and as a result an explosion was averted. Men had a chance to testify to the "outrage" that had been perpetrated on them, speakers had an opportunity to shout their anathema at the committee and to warn those responsible of the wrath to come. Some had a chance to demand a roll-call, and a few availed themselves of the privilege of saying, "Mr. Chairman, Mr. Chairman, I demand to poll the delegation," and then the engine gave two toots, the conductor waved his lantern, and the well-oiled machine lunged forward.

There is nothing like debate to smooth out the troubles of a convention. The man who invented gag law did not understand the pacifying influence of sound as it passes out of the throat. Some scientist has announced the startling theory that anger is a poison that is relieved by swearing. I am not willing to accept the theory without more proof than has yet been presented, but I am firmly convinced, by long attendance at conventions, that there are few sorrows of a political nature that free discussion cannot heal. Even where satisfaction is not guaranteed a long contest, like a spirited campaign, makes the contestants willing to accept almost anything if they can only get through.

It looks now as if the Taft forces were in a position to dictate the terms of surrender, and there seems little likelihood of the President's withdrawing in favor of a compromise candidate. I am prepared to offer a certain amount of consolation to whichever candidate is defeated, but my cautious and conservative nature makes me hesitate to pronounce a eulogy until the corpse is identified.

Looking back upon the struggle from the standpoint of an outsider I have been able to watch the contest with impartiality. Having felt the force of the united influence of the two principals, I have been able to bear with greater fortitude the falling out that has converted two bosom friends into bitter enemies. Not being attached to them as closely as they have been to each other, I do not feel as keenly as they do what each calls ingratitude in the other. I have weighed their public acts, or tried to, with fairness, anxious to give each one credit for any good that he has accomplished. I have tried to be charitable to their faults, recognizing that we all have shortcomings and need to have charity extended to us.

"Nothing succeeds like success"; the change of a vote may convert a defeat into a victory, and then those fawn and flatter who would have turned away in the hour of darkness.

If Mr. Taft wins in this convention there will be plenty to bring him bouquets, and he will not notice it if none of them bears my card. Mr. Roosevelt will, in that case, be the one who will be in need of kind words, and I shall take pleasure in calling attention to some of the substantial benefits he has conferred upon the country. He has yet the possibility of leadership in a new party, if the Democratic party should disappoint the hopes of the progressives of the country and surrender itself to the service of Wall Street.

If, on the other hand, the boiler blows up, or the machine breaks down, and Mr. Taft is defeated, there are compliments which I can pay him, and pay him with pleasure. In that case it would be much easier for me to get to him, and he would appreciate it more, than it would be to get within speaking distance of the ex-president surrounded by a "We want Teddy" crowd. My last article on this convention will deal, therefore, with the platform adopted and with the virtues of the deceased.

XIII

THE END OF THE CONVENTION

Mr. Bryan's letter in morning newspapers of Sunday, June 23d.

On the Train from Chicago to Baltimore, June 22.—The break has come, and the progressives were happy in their selection of the time. They waited until the credentials committee had made its last report, until the committee-made majority had voted itself the convention, until it was demonstrated that no amount of fact or argument availed to reverse the decisions based upon the exigencies of the case rather than upon the merits of the contest, and then Delegate Allen, of Kansas, read Mr. Roosevelt's statement and enforced its pungent paragraphs with pointed remarks of his own.

As Mr. Roosevelt's statement is published on a later page I need make no reference to it here. It will prove a historic document. Never before in American politics has a convention witnessed such a scene—a man, one of the most forceful figures of his time, twice a president, once by the accident of death and once by the largest majority ever given to a president, contending against an administration that he created for the honor of a Republican nomination.

In spite of patronage, in spite of the powerful organization of a dominant party and in spite of great commercial influences, he actually secures an undisputed majority of the Republican vote. Contrary to all precedents he goes to the convention city and conducts his own fight. He finds himself hedged about by forces with which he cannot cope. If he may be likened to a caged lion confined in a cage constructed of regularity, formality and orderly procedure, it must be admitted that he was unable, with all his Samson-like strength, to bend a single bar.

But here the simile ends. Man is more than an animal. He laughs at the limitations of the flesh. He can appeal to a power greater than the politician, and Mr. Roosevelt has made his appeal. He brings against the convention such an indictment as no party has ever had to meet before. He appeals from leaders inebriated by prolonged power, to the voters who can dispassionately weigh policies and measure methods from Philip drunk to Philip sober.

The platform is such a platform as might be expected for Mr. Taft. It points with pride to what he has done and views with alarm all that Mr.

Roosevelt stands for and threatens to do. The curious may read it, but it will play a very small part in the campaign. In the Republican mind Mr. Taft has come to stand for stand-patism and Mr. Roosevelt for progressivism, and the voters will not make any nice calculations in deciding between them.

The Republican party is passing through the same convulsions which the Democratic party passed through sixteen years ago, when progressive Democracy was born. In the case of our party, the mother lived. At present both a physician and a surgeon are in attendance, and it will be some months before the fate of the patient will be known.

I was compelled to leave just before former Vice-President Fairbanks concluded reading the platform, but, from what had taken place, the renomination of the President seemed a foregone conclusion.

As was to be expected, the Chicago convention will exert a marked influence upon the Democratic convention about to begin at Baltimore. The fact that more than half of the Republican party has been shown to be militant in its progressiveness would seem to make it even more imperatively necessary than before that the Democratic convention should, in its platform and with its nominations, respond to the demands of the progressives of the nation and thus make a third party unnecessary. This is the way it looks from a distance. I can make a better forecast after reaching Baltimore.

THE WITHDRAWAL OF THE ROOSEVELT DELEGATES

It was Henry J. Allen, of Kansas, who in a speech announced the intention of the Roosevelt delegates to take no further active part in the convention. He said the first thing he desired permission for was to read a statement which had just been placed in his hands from Theodore Roosevelt. Mr. Allen then read the following statement:

" 'A clear majority of the delegates honestly elected to this convention were chosen by the people to nominate me. Under the direction, and with the encouragement of Mr. Taft, the majority of the national committee, by the so-called "steam-roller" methods, and with scandalous disregard of every principle of elementary honesty and decency, stole eighty or ninety delegates, putting on the temporary roll-call a sufficient number of fraudulent delegates to defeat the legally expressed will of the people, and to substitute a dishonest for an honest majority.

" 'The convention has now declined to purge the roll of the fraudulent delegates placed thereon by the defunct national committee, and the majority which thus indorsed fraud was made a majority only because it included the fraudulent delegates themselves, who all sat as judges on one another's cases. If these fraudulent votes had not thus been cast and counted the convention would have been purged of their presence. This action makes the convention in no proper sense any longer a Republican convention representing the real Republican party. Therefore I hope the men elected as Roosevelt delegates will now decline to vote on any matter before the convention. I do not release any delegate from his

MR. BRYAN'S DEPARTURE FROM THE REPUBLICAN CONVENTION TO GO TO BALTIMORE.

(*McCutcheon in "Collier's Weekly." Reproduced by Permission.*)

The standing figure is Former Vice-President Fairbanks, who is reading the platform. The Chicago "Tribune," in describing the scene, says that when Mr. Fairbanks had got about half through Mr. Bryan got up from his seat in the press stand and started for the door. Instantly the galleries began to cheer him. The applause was so insistent that Mr. Fairbanks finally was compelled to stop. Even Chairman Root's gavel could not stop the din, and it continued until the Democratic leader had passed out of sight through one of the exits.

honorable obligation to vote for me if he votes at all, but under the actual conditions I hope that he will not vote at all.

" 'The convention as now composed has no claim to represent the voters of the Republican party. It represents nothing but successful fraud in overriding the will of the rank and file of the party. Any man nominated by the convention as now constituted would be merely the beneficiary of this successful fraud; it would be deeply discreditable to any man to accept the convention's nomination under these circumstances; and any man thus accepting it would have no claim to the support of any Republican on party grounds, and would have forfeited the right to ask the support of any honest man of any party on moral grounds.

" 'THEODORE ROOSEVELT.' "

Mr. Allen then proceeded to say:

"We have reached a point where a majority of the Roosevelt delegates feel that they can no longer share in the responsibility for the acts of this convention. We have contended with you until we have exhausted every parliamentary privilege in an effort to have placed upon the roll the names of men legally elected.

"When by using the votes of the delegates whose rights to sit in this convention are challenged, you took a position which places the power of a political committee above the authority of 77,000 majority, elected in a legal primary in California, we decided that your steam roller had exceeded the speed limit. Since then we have asked for no roll-call. You have now completed the seating of all contested delegates, using the votes of the contested delegates to accomplish your purpose. * * *

"We will not put ourselves in a position to be bound by any act in which you say to the majority who rejected Mr. Taft in New Jersey, to the majority who rejected him in Wisconsin, to the majority who rejected him in Minnesota, to the majority who rejected him in Maine, to the majority who rejected him in Maryland, to the majority in South Dakota, to the majority in North Dakota, which gave him only 1,500 votes out of 59,000; to the majorities which rejected him in Nebraska, in Oregon, Minnesota, Kansas, Oklahoma, West Virginia and North Carolina, that all these majorities added together went down under the mere rulings of a political committee.

"We will not join you in saying to the home State of Abraham Lincoln that the 150,000 majority with which you defeated Mr. Taft and his managers in Illinois was overruled by those very managers with the consent of those who have arrogated powers never intended to be theirs.

"When Theodore Roosevelt left the White House four years ago he left you an overwhelming majority in both branches of Congress; he left you an overwhelming majority in all the great Republican States; he left you a record upon which you could elect Mr. Taft; he left you a progressive program to carry forward. That program was buried beneath an avalanche of words at Winona, and eighteen Republican governors were buried beneath an avalanche of votes which rebuked recreancy to party pledges.

"We will not participate with you in completing the scuttling of the ship. We will not say to the young men of the nation, who, reading political history with their patriotism, and longing to catch step with the party of their fathers, that we have nothing better to offer them at this hour than this new declaration of human rights—that a discarded political committee, as its last act, holds greater power than a majority of over 2,000,000 voters.

"We do not bolt. We merely insist that you, not we, are making the record. And we refuse to be bound by it. We have pleaded with you for ten days. We have fought with you five days for a 'square deal.' We fight no more. We plead no longer. We shall sit in protest and the people who sent us here shall judge us.

"You accuse us of being radical. Gentlemen, let me tell you that no radical in the ranks of radicalism ever did so radical a thing as to come to a national convention of the great Republican party and secure through fraud the nomination of a man that they know could not be elected."

XIV

THE REPUBLICAN PLATFORM

The Republican party, assembled by its representatives in national convention, declares its unchanging faith in government of the people, by the people, for the people. We renew our allegiance to the principles of the Republican party and our devotion to the cause of Republican institutions established by the fathers.

It is appropriate that we should now recall with a sense of veneration and gratitude the name of our first great leader who was nominated in this city, and whose lofty principles and superb devotion to his country are an inspiration to the party he honored—Abraham Lincoln. In the present state of public affairs we should be inspired by his broad statesmanship and by his tolerant spirit toward men.

* * *

The Republican party is opposed to special privilege and to monopoly. It placed upon the statute book the interstate commerce act of 1887, and the important amendments thereto, and the antitrust act of 1890, and it has consistently and successfully enforced the provisions of these laws. It will take no backward step to permit the reëstablishment in any degree of conditions which were intolerable.

Experience makes it plain that the business of the country may be carried on without fear or without disturbance, and at the same time without resort to practices which are abhorrent to the common sense of justice.

The Republican party favors the enactment of legislation supplementary to the existing antitrust act which will define as criminal offenses those specific acts that uniformly mark attempts to restrain and to monopolize trade to the end that those who honestly intend to obey the law may have a guide for their action, and that those who aim to violate the law may the more surely be punished.

The same certainty should be given to the law prohibiting combinations and monopolies that characterizes other provisions of commercial law, in order that no part of the field of business opportunity may be restricted by monopoly or combination, that business success honorably achieved may not be converted into crime, and that the right of every man to acquire commodities, and particularly the necessaries of life, in an open market uninfluenced by the manipulation of trust or combination may be preserved.

* *

We reaffirm our belief in a protective tariff. The

Republican tariff policy has been of the greatest benefit to the country, developing our resources, diversifying our industries, and protecting our workmen against competition with cheaper labor abroad, thus establishing for our wage earners the American standard of living.

The protective tariff is so woven into the fabric of our industrial and agricultural life that to substitute for it a tariff for revenue only would destroy many industries and throw millions of our people out of employment. The products of the farm and of the mine should receive the same measure of protection as other products of American labor.

We hold that the import duties should be high enough while yielding a sufficient revenue to protect adequately American industries and wages. Some of the existing import duties are too high, and should be reduced. Readjustment should be made from time to time to conform to changed conditions and to reduce excessive rates, but without injury to any American industry.

To accomplish this correct information is indispensable. This information can best be obtained by an expert commission, as the large volume of useful facts contained in the recent reports of the tariff board has demonstrated.

The pronounced feature of modern industrial life is its enormous diversification. To apply tariff rates justly to these changing conditions requires closer study and more scientific methods than ever before. The Republican party has shown by its creation of a tariff board its recognition of this situation and its determination to be equal to it.

We condemn the Democratic party for its failure to either provide funds for the continuance of this board or to make some other provision for securing the information requisite for intelligent tariff legislation. We protest against the Democratic method of legislating on these important subjects without careful investigation.

We condemn the Democratic tariff bills passed by the house of representatives of the Sixty-second congress as sectional, as injurious to the public credit, and as destructive of business enterprise.

The steadily increasing cost of living has become a matter not only of national but of worldwide concern. The fact that it is not due to the protective tariff system is evidenced by the existence of similar conditions in countries which have a tariff policy different from our own, as well as by the fact that the cost of living has increased while rates of duty have remained stationary or been reduced.

The Republican party will support a prompt scientific inquiry into the causes which are operative, both in the United States and elsewhere, to increase the cost of living. When the exact facts are known it will take the necessary steps to remove any abuses that may be found to exist, in order that the cost of the food, clothing, and shelter of the people may in no way be unduly or artificially increased.

* *

It is of great importance to the social and economic welfare of this country that its farmers have facilities for borrowing easily and cheaply the money they need to increase the productivity of their land.

It is as important that financial machinery be provided to supply the demand of farmers for credit as it is that the banking and currency systems be reformed in the interest of general business.

Therefore, we recommend and urge an authoritative investigation of agricultural credit societies and corporations in other countries, and the passage of state and federal laws for the establishment and capable supervision of organizations having for their purpose the loaning of funds to farmers.

* *

We favor such additional legislation as may be necessary more effectively to prohibit corporations from contributing funds, directly or indirectly, to campaigns for the nomination or election of the president, the vice president, senators, and representatives in congress.

We heartily approve the recent act of congress requiring the fullest publicity in regard to all campaign contributions, whether made in connection with primaries, conventions, or elections.

We rejoice in the success of the distinctive Republican policy of the conservation of our national resources for their use by the people without waste and without monopoly. We pledge ourselves to a continuance of such a policy.

We favor such fair and reasonable rules and regulations as will not discourage or interfere with actual bona fide homeseekers, prospectors, and miners in the acquisition of public lands under existing laws.

In the interest of the general public, and particularly of the agricultural or rural communities, we favor legislation looking to the establishment, under proper regulations, of a parcels post, the postal rates to be graduated under a zone similar in proportion to the length of carriage.

We approve the action taken by the president and the congress to secure with Russia, as with other countries, a treaty that will recognize the absolute right of expatriation and that will prevent all discrimination of whatever kind between American citizens, whether native born or alien and regardless of race, religion, or previous political allegiance. The right of asylum is a precious possession of the people of the United States, and it is to be neither surrendered nor restricted.

* *

The Mississippi river is the nation's drainage ditch. Its flood waters gathered from thirty-one states and the Dominion of Canada, constitute an overpowering force which breaks the levees and pours its torrents over many million acres of the richest land in the union, stopping mails, impeding commerce, and causing great loss of life and property.

These floods are national in scope and the disasters they produce seriously affect the general welfare. The state unaided cannot cope with this giant problem, hence we believe the federal government should assume a fair proportion of the burden of its control so as to prevent the disasters from recurring floods.

We favor the continuance of the policy of the government with regard to the reclamation of arid lands; and for the encouragement of the speedy settlement and improvement of such lands we favor an amendment to the law that will reasonably extend the time within which the cost of any reclamation project may be repaid by the land owners under it.

We pledge the Republican party to the enactment of appropriate laws to give relief from the constantly growing evil of induced or undesirable immigration which is inimical to the progress and welfare of the people of the United States.

We favor the speedy enactment of laws to provide that seamen shall not be compelled to endure involuntary servitude, and that life and property at sea shall be safeguarded by the ample equipment of vessels with life saving appliances and with full complements of skilled, able bodied seamen to operate them.

The approaching completion of the Panama canal, the establishment of a bureau of mines, the institution of postal savings banks, the increased provision made in 1912 for the aged and infirm soldiers and sailors of the republic and for their widows, and the vigorous administration of the laws relating to pure food and drugs all mark the successful progress of Republican administration, and are additional evidence of its effectiveness.

* *

We challenge successful criticism of the sixteen years of Republican administration under Presidents McKinley, Roosevelt, and Taft. We heartily reaffirm the indorsement of President McKinley contained in the platform of 1900 and of 1904, and that of President Roosevelt contained in the platform of 1904 and 1908.

We invite the intelligent judgment of the American people upon the administration of William H. Taft. The country has prospered and been at peace under his presidency. During the years in which he had the coöperation of a Republican congress an unexampled amount of constructive legislation was framed and passed in the interest of the people, and in obedience to their wish. That legislation is a record on which any administration might appeal with confidence to the favorable judgment of history.

We appeal to the American electorate upon the record of the Republican party and upon this declaration of its principles and purposes. We are confident that under the leadership of the candidates here to be nominated our appeal will not be in vain; that the Republican party will meet every just expectation of the people whose servant it is; that under its administration and its laws our nation will continue to advance; that peace and prosperity will abide with the people, and that new glory will be added to the great republic.

XV

A CRITICISM OF MR. TAFT'S SPEECH OF ACCEPTANCE

(Mr. Bryan's Article in Morning Newspapers of August 3.)

President Taft's speech of acceptance will for several reasons stand out in Presidential history as a very remarkable public utterance. To begin with, he accepts Senator Root's guarantee of regularity without a smile, and even adds his indorsement of the proceedings which resulted in his nomination. This occasion he says is appropriate for the expression of profound gratitude at the victory for the right which was won at Chicago.

By that victory the Republican party was saved for future usefulness. What an astounding indifference to the intelligence of the public! How completely has his conscience been seared not to be sensitive in regard to the methods employed at Chicago. Both he and Senator Root know that he was not the choice of a majority of the Republican voters; they know that the President's Administration was repudiated by those who elected him.

They know that a holdover committee deliberately and contemptuously disregarded the voters of the party and changed the character of the convention by the seating of Taft delegates.

Holdover committeemen who had been repudiated in their States knowingly, even exultingly, thwarted the expressed will of the Republican voters of their respective States in order to give an apparent indorsement to the Administration, and President Taft is willing to accept this shadow as if it were substantial.

The President knows that the Republican committeemen from a number of Southern States represent mythical constituencies, and he accepts with expressions of gratitude a nomination that was only possible because Southern Republicans had many times as much influence in the convention in proportion to their number as Northern Republicans had. And he accepts the nomination without any suggestions as to improvement in method. He neither indorses the Baltimore plan of having committeemen begin to serve as soon as elected, thus having a new committee organize a convention, nor does he outline any plan for protecting the Republican party from the scandal brought upon its conventions by its patronage-controlled delegates from the Southern States.

The next thing in the President's speech that attracts attention is the marked contrast between his point of view to-day and his point of view four years ago. In 1908 he was condemning the malefactors of great wealth and crying out against dishonest methods in business. He held himself out as a reformer, and appealed to the progressive sentiment of the country.

Now he is horrified at the demagogue, the muckraker and the political disturber. He says that in the work of rousing the people to the danger that threatened our civilization, from the abuses of concentrated wealth and the power it was likely to exercise, the public imagination was wrought upon and a reign of sensational journalism and unjust and unprincipled muckraking has followed in which much injustice has been done to honest men.

Demagogues have seized the opportunity to further inflame the public mind, and have sought to turn the peculiar conditions to their advantage. He contends that it is far better to await the diminution of this evil by natural causes than to attempt what would soon take on the aspect of confiscation or to abolish the principle or institution of private property and to change to socialism.

What a difference in the tone of the two speeches! Four years ago he was alarmed for fear the country was going to suffer at the hands of the predatory interests; now every exploiter is pleasing and only the reformer is vile. His speech of four years ago must have been delivered during a mental aberration. Surgeons tell us that a man's eccentricities are sometimes due to a pressure on the brain at some point. It is possible that Doctors Root, Penrose and Barnes have restored his mind to normal action by removing the Roosevelt pressure.

Mr. Taft is so solicitous about the people who have failed to devote as much time as is necessary to political duties that he is afraid to burden them with responsibilities three times greater than the people have been willing to assume. He is afraid that to concede the reforms demanded will result in new duties that will tire them (the people) into such an indifference as still further to demand control of public affairs by a mere minority. To find an argument as absurd as the above one must go back several centuries and consult the reasons that kings gave for not admitting the people to participation in government, and then, to add insult to injury, he has the audacity to present the aristocratic argument that it is bread, not votes, that the people need; work, not constitutional amendments; money to pay house rent, not referendums; clothing, not recalls; employment, not initiatives.

Modern literature presents no parallel to this ignorance of or indifference to the growth of popular government. In referring to reforms that come under his Administration he confines himself to a few, and these are not the most important.

Why does he ignore the popular election of United States Senators? It is the greatest reform in methods of government that has come since the adoption of our Constitution. Why does he overlook it? Is it because it came without his aid?

Why does he fail to mention the income tax amendment to the Constitution? He urged it in a message, but he did it in order to defeat a statutory income tax, and he has never said a word since then to encourage its ratification by the States.

He even appointed Gov. Hughes to the Supreme Court bench after the latter had sent a message to the New York Legislature opposing the ratification of the income tax amendment.

Why is he silent on the publicity law passed in the interest of pure politics? Was it because the publicity before the election provided for in the law which he was compelled to sign rebuked his utterances of 1908, when he insisted that contributions should not be made public until after election?

Here are three great reforms that have come during his administration, and yet he cannot claim credit for any of them, although, but for his reason for recommending it, he might claim some credit for the income tax amendment. He defends the Payne-Aldrich bill; says it has vindicated itself.

He praises the Supreme Court decision writing the word "unreasonable" into the anti-trust law—a decision which made every trust magnate rejoice. He eulogizes the dissolution, falsely so-called, of the Oil and Tobacco Trusts—a dissolution that leaves the trusts undisturbed and has already increased the value of their stocks—and he advocates Federal incorporation of big business, the one thing that the trusts still need to complete their control of the industries of the country.

What a program at a time like this when three-fourths of the voters of the country are up in arms against the plunderbund! Not content with an indorsement of everything reactionary that Wall Street has had the courage to suggest he threatens panic if anything is done to disturb those who fatten on Governmental favoritism and legislative privilege.

He even appeals to Democrats to join him in an earnest effort to avert the political and economic revolution and business paralysis which Republican defeat will bring about.

The President's defense of his refusal to intervene in Mexico is the best thing in his speech, but his reference to China gives weight to the rumor that recognition of the Republic of China is being withheld as a means of forcing upon China the acceptance of an American loan. He says on this subject:

"We have lent our good offices in the negotiation of a loan essential to the continuance of the Republic and which China will accept." If this is an admission that his Administration is attempting to compel China to borrow from our financiers as a condition precedent of the recognition of the Republic he confesses to an inexcusable degradation of the Department of State.

Democrats will resent the President's action in associating them with the progressive Republicans. In replying to the former Republicans, as he calls them in one place, and to those who have left the Republican party, as he calls them in another place in his speech, he replies to Democrats also and accuses both groups of going in a direction they do not definitely know; toward an end they cannot definitely describe, with but one chief and clear object—and that is acquiring power for their parties by popular support through a promise of a change for the better.

This is a very unfair statement of the Democratic position in view of the fact that the Democratic platform is the only one that is specific in pointing out abuses and in proposing remedies, and in view of the further fact that the Democratic party has shown its fidelity to the people by its willingness to suffer defeat in its advocacy of the reforms which are now being accepted by the entire country.

The President pays himself a high compliment when he offers himself to the voters as the only exponent of constitutional government. He, as well as the Roosevelt party, aver that the Democratic party is not to be trusted to preserve the Constitution, and he declares that this is to him the supreme issue.

The Republican party, he declares, is the nucleus of that public opinion which favors consistent progress and development along safe and sane lines and under the Constitution, as we have had it for more than one hundred years, &c.

Here, then, is the paramount issue: Shall the Constitution be preserved by President Taft with such aid as he can secure from Root, Penrose, Barnes, Lorimer, and the other self-appointed custodians of constitutional government? Shall our organic law be given over into the hands of those who favor the election of Senators by the people, the income tax amendment, a single term for the President, and other changes of this character which have for their object the divorcing of government from the favor-seeking, privilege-hunting classes?

If this is to be the supreme issue, the Democrats are ready to call the battle on.

Part Two

THE DEMOCRATIC NATIONAL CONVENTION
BALTIMORE, JUNE 25–JULY 2, 1912

I

THE TWO CONTENDING FACTIONS

Mr. Bryan's letter in morning newspapers of Monday, June 24th.

Baltimore, June 23.—The convention opens here with a situation somewhat like that in Chicago—like it in the fact that there are two elements in the party, each represented by its leaders. The progressive is here in force, but the reactionary is here also.

There has been no test vote in the national committee since the vote in the Guffey case. At that time the national committee stood thirty for Guffey and eighteen for Palmer. The reactionaries claim that fairly represents the lineup between the two elements. Since the Guffey case was decided several changes have been made in the national committee. Guffey himself has gone out and Congressman Palmer has taken his place. Mr. Johnson of Texas has gone out and Caleb Sells has taken his place.

There are other changes, but the new members do not begin to act until the permanent organization is completed, and it is not certain that a reactionary committeeman would give expression to the changed sentiment in his state.

The subcommittee decided by a vote of eight to eight to recommend Alton B. Parker for temporary chairman. The eight against Judge Parker were divided as follows: Three for James, three for Henry, one for Kern, and one for O'Gorman. This gave Parker a plurality, but not a majority. The recommendation will be taken up to-morrow by the full committee, and the committee's recommendation will be approved or disapproved. The action of the full committee will then come before the convention for acceptance or rejection.

The Clark men supported James and the Wilson men for the most part supported Henry. If the eight could have agreed upon a progressive it would have been a tie vote, but the friends of the different candidates were anxious, of course, to secure whatever advantage they could for their candidate, and hence the muddle. An effort is being made by the progressives to secure an agreement upon some candidate. I am not prepared to predict what the full committee will do, but I think a poll should be taken.

In fighting for a principle it ought not to make any difference whether many or few rally around the standard. It is better to make a fight for the **right** and lose than to concede a thing that is

ATLAS.

(*C. R. Macauley in the New York "World."*)

wrong. A beginning has to be made some time, and the sooner it is made the better.

Then, too, no one can tell until the vote is counted what the result will be. There are many who will promise to vote one way in order to prevent a vote, who will vote the opposite way if they have to vote. It is in recognition of this that our constitutions require a roll-call and every one acquainted with parliamentary practice knows that motions often carry by a viva voce vote that are lost on roll-call.

If a majority of the national committee votes in favor of Judge Parker, the opposition will be carried to the floor of the convention and the delegates will have a chance to go on record and that record will mean a great deal both to the delegates and to the party.

The objection to Judge Parker is not personal. No one, so far as I know, has any ill-feeling against him. The objection made to him is based upon the fact that he stands as the most conspicuous representative of the reactionary element of the party. He was the man chosen by the so-called conservative element of the party to lead the fight in 1904, when the party receded from the advanced position it had taken in 1896 and 1900.

The Wall street influence dominated our organization that year and put its brand upon our campaign. Belmont and Ryan were the financial sponsors of the party. When the compaign was over and the vote counted it was found Judge Parker had polled about a million and a quarter less votes than the party polled in 1896 and 1900, and I may add, a million and a quarter votes less than the party polled four years afterward.

It is only fair to Judge Parker to say that his failure to poll the party vote was not due to lack of personal popularity, but to the influences that dominated his campaign. It would be impossible to separate him at this time from the influences that gave character to his campaign then. He is the choice now of the men who then spoke for him. He is urged upon the committee by Mr. Murphy and he is supported by those who are responsive to the influence which speak through Mr. Murphy. His selection as temporary chairman would be an announcement to the public that the convention is a reactionary convention. It might make all the professions it liked; it might talk as it would about progressiveness, but what it said would not atone for what it did. Actions often speak louder than words.

This convention is progressive; at least it is supposed to be. The two leading candidates are progressive. The chief contention of the friends of either has been that he has more progressiveness than the other. It has been a race to see which could progress the more rapidly, but neither candidate could have any substantial following on any other platform.

These two candidates together have instructed delegates to the extent of nearly two-thirds of the convention. To put up the chief of reactionaries to open a progressive convention with a stand-pat keynote is an insult that is not likely to go unrebuked unless we are mistaken in the character of the members of this convention, and if we are mistaken, the sooner we find it out the better.

If our convention had been held before the Chicago convention it would have been necessary to adopt a progressive platform and nominate a progressive ticket in response to an overwhelming sentiment in the party. But now that the Republican party has acted, it has become a matter of expediency as well as a matter of principle to leave no doubt in the public mind as to our party's attitude on the great issues that now divide the country.

Circumstances have brought victory to our very doors; it would be madness to invite repudiation at the polls by compromise with predatory interests. I cannot believe that such a result is possible. What a pity that harmony should be disturbed at the very beginning of this convention by an impudent attempt upon the part of the special interests to get control of the convention and represent the party! What a pity that the lesson recently taught at Chicago should have had so little effect on those who are seeking to paralyze the party's efforts as a reform party!

When the Republican party adjourned yesterday it had by its actions changed the first and second lines of "Auld Lang Syne" to read:

> Let old acquaintance be forgot
> And never brought to mind.

It looks as if the same influences that dominated the Chicago convention are attempting to open this convention with the familiar lines: "Hail! Hail! The gang's all here."

II

THE FIGHT FOR A PROGRESSIVE CHAIRMAN

Mr. Bryan's article in afternoon papers of Monday, June 24th.

Baltimore, June 24.—The morning's developments have been few. The delegates are arriving and opening headquarters. The most prominent arrival this morning was Governor Burke, of North Dakota. He has the support of his state for the presidency, and at once aligned himself with the progressive fight against Judge Parker for temporary chairman.

He brought his answer to my telegram and delivered it in person. Governor Burke has been elected for a third term in his state, and his popularity is due to his strength as an executive and to the satisfaction which his administrations have given. He is one of the strong men in our party, and is not only favorably considered for the office of president, but will doubtless have a still larger support for the vice presidency, if geographical conditions do not weigh against him.

The national committee is in session, having under consideration the question of temporary chairman. The progressives are still engaged in an endeavor to get together on some candidate with some prospect of success. The Wall street influence is on hand, stiffening the back of Judge Parker's supporters, but the tide seems to be turning more strongly against Parker as the delegates arrive.

I do not like to discuss my part in the convention, and yet I am compelled to do so or deny this information to those who read these reports. I will therefore say that I am not attending the meeting of the full committee, preferring to leave them to agree upon a progressive without suggestion from me, if they can do so.

If they fail to do so and Judge Parker is recommended by the full committee, I shall from the floor of the convention oppose his selection and propose the name of some progressive as a substitute for his. I do not know who that progressive will be and I shall not decide until the last moment, my sole desire being to bring about harmonious cooperation between the friends of the progressive candidate and any one upon whom they can agree will have my hearty support.

If they cannot agree I will then take the responsibility of finding a progressive to present as a candidate—the best one whose consent is obtainable. If I fail in my effort to find a candidate, I shall myself be a candidate, in order that those who are attending the convention may have an opportunity to vote for a temporary chairman whose speech will indorse the party's progressive record, and urge an advance along progressive lines.

The discussion of candidates is for the time being suspended. Until we find out what kind of a convention this is no forecast can be made. If it is shown to be a reactionary convention the interest in the presidential nomination will probably decline, for it will not make much difference who carries the standard if the party centers into competition with the Taft party for the support of predatory interests.

(*Report of an Interview with Mr. Bryan on Sunday Night, June 23, as Printed in "The Chicago Tribune" of June 24.*)

Mr. Bryan, in an interview given nearly 100 newspaper men, made it clear that he regarded the fight for the temporary chairmanship one where progressivism and conservatism were the issues.

He would not throw any light on what plans he had made to oppose the selection of A. B. Parker, whom he charged with being a reactionary. He flatly asserted that to begin a progressive convention with a reactionary speech would be an offense to the Democratic party.

Mr. Bryan was asked if he had any particular candidate for temporary chairman of the convention in place of Mr. Parker.

"I do not care to discuss the matter," he said, "except

to say that any progressive will be satisfactory to me. In the first place, I urged the committee to consult with the two leading candidates and allow them to determine upon a satisfactory temporary chairman."

"Do you regard Wilson and Clark as the two leading candidates?"

"Do you know of anybody else?" he answered.

"Yes, I meant Wilson and Clark and if they had agreed upon a temporary chairman there would have been no objection whatsoever.

"I want to emphasize one fact right here," Mr. Bryan continued, "and that is, that I am the original harmony man in this whole crowd. I did not ask anything for myself; I did not ask anything for any particular candidate. I do not know of any better way of beginning the convention harmoniously than to have the two leading candidates agree upon a temporary chairman.

"If there is any lack of harmony I do not see why there should be any excitement about the matter. Eight members of the committee have seen fit to ignore the opinions of the other eight and to make the recommendation.

"It takes the full committee to decide whether to approve or disapprove the recommendation of the subcommittee and it is for the convention to decide whether it will accept or reject the recommendation. It is not an unprecedented thing for a committee's recommendation to be rejected. It was rejected in the Chicago convention in 1896."

"Would not such an action here precipitate a fight which would be detrimental to the party?"

"It precipitated a fight then," he answered. "And let me add that our party is better for the fight. It saved the party from disgrace. When I say 'disgrace,' I mean that to begin a progressive convention with a reactionary speech would be an offense to the party of the nation."

"How are you going to conduct a fight for a progressive unless you have some particular candidate in view?"

"It has been stated that you cannot have a contest between two men until you have the men, but I had no disposition to select the man at all. I simply urged the committee to ascertain, if possible, the man upon whom the two leading candidates could agree."

"Will there be any split in the Democratic party?"

"I have no knowledge on that subject."

"Well, can you imagine a progressive program being repudiated here as in Chicago?"

"No," he replied, "for I cannot imagine so large a Wall street element in our party as they had in Chicago."

"They say you are going to bolt if you are defeated in this matter, as Roosevelt did in Chicago."

"I am not responsible for what they are saying. My friends are not saying that.

"I think the outcome of the Chicago convention," continued Mr. Bryan, "makes it even more imperative that we should in this convention write a progressive platform and nominate a progressive ticket."

"Mr. Hall of your State said you would not bolt. Could there be any circumstances under which you would feel justified in doing so?"

"My dear sir," answered Mr. Bryan, "I have always avoided hypothetical questions since 1896. At that time an opponent put a hypothetical question to an expert on insanity, describing me as he saw me, and then asked whether such a man was insane, and the expert answered that he undoubtedly was."

"There were four names considered by the committee for the temporary chairmanship. Would any of the others be acceptable to you?"

"Yes, any progressive would be perfectly acceptable," answered Mr. Bryan.

III

THE STEAM ROLLER AT WORK

Mr. Bryan's letter in morning newspapers of Tuesday, June 25th.

Baltimore, June 24.—Baltimore is to be a little Chicago. We have the same steam roller here, only of a smaller pattern, but the employees are skilled laborers and they have the machine in perfect running order. The "toot, toot" will be heard as soon as the chairman calls the convention to order and it will continue until the convention adjourns sine die, unless the delegates rise in their might and throw it in the scrap heap.

I have attended conventions since my youth, but I have never known a more brazen attempt upon the part of an insignificant few to thwart the will of the rank and file of the party than may be seen here. It is not burglary, but plain open daylight robbery, where the leaders do not even take the trouble to wear masks.

If the plain every day citizen, who earns his bread in the sweat of his brow, could understand the influences that operate at a convention like this; if he could see the misrepresentatives of the people slipping around to the rooms of those who manipulate the schemes through which the public is plundered; if he could number the whispered conversations that take place in dark corners; if he could hear the specious arguments made in behalf of regularity; if he could be made aware of the tremendous pressure that is brought to bear on the weak, and of the deceptions practiced upon the unsuspecting, he would realize how important it is that men should be selected as delegates whose hearts are right, whose sympathies are with the people, and who have the moral courage to stand for the silent masses.

It is safe to say that four fifths of the Democratic party is progressive. Every Democrat who announced himself as a candidate for the presidency claimed to be a progressive. There is not one single piece of literature circulated among Democrats that represented as reactionary the candidate in whose interest it was issued. And yet all at once we find that quite a number of delegates elected as progressives and instructed for progressives are reactionary in their sympathies.

What candidate could have secured the instructions of a single state west of New York or south of the Potomac if he had announced that Judge Parker represented his idea of Democracy and that he would ask Judge Parker to open the campaign

TRYING TO SQUARE IT WITH THE PEERLESS LEADER.
(*McCutcheon in the Chicago "Tribune."*)

with a keynote speech? It is not complimentary to the intelligence of a constituency for a delegate to suppose that the Democrats who have borne the burden in the sixteen year struggle are unacquainted with Judge Parker and the kind of Democracy he stands for.

They know how he was nominated at St. Louis. They know how he repudiated the party platform after the nomination; they know the collapse of his campaign; they know how Wall street at the last moment turned against him after having by its support of him driven the masses from him; they know of the widespread overthrow of Democratic strongholds; they know the indignation that was felt among Democrats when they fully realized the cause of their discomfiture; they know how local offices were turned over to the Republicans in a multitude of districts; they know what an effort it required to wash from the party's banner the stain that his candidacy put upon it, and they understand the significance of the return of his friends to control in the party.

It is little less than a tragedy to shatter the hopes that millions of Democrats have been encouraged to cherish. The principles for which progressive Democracy has been contending have grown astonishingly within the last few years.

Ex-President Roosevelt has been able to marshal considerably more than half of the Republican voters around his standard because he has scathingly denounced the plunderbund, the subsidized press, the corrupt boss, and the conscienceless misrepresentation of the voters by those who assumed to speak for them. He only waits the capture of this convention by the same influences to justify the organization of a third party and lead to defeat both divisions of plutocracy's army, if as the result of this convention he can show that the Democratic party is identical with the Republican party in the forces in control.

The national committee, by the vote of 32 for Parker, 20 for James, and 2 for O'Gorman, indorsed the action of the subcommittee, several of the Parker votes coming from committeemen whose delegations asked them to vote against Parker, or whose delegations are known to be against Parker.

Will the convention ratify the action of the committee and invite the protest of the voters of the party? We shall know a little after noon tomorrow.

IV

FINANCIAL INTERESTS AT WÔRK

(Mr. Bryan's Article in Afternoon Papers of Tuesday, June 25th.)

Baltimore, June 25.—The forenoon is being occupied with caucuses and canvasses. The lines are being drawn.

Now that the delegates are learning that Murphy is but the heavy hand of Ryan, they are thinking of what their constituents will say if this convention is delivered to the same financial interests that controlled the Chicago convention, through Root and his machine.

It is a spectacle never before witnessed in American politics. Two conventions of opposing parties meeting within two weeks, and the same financial jugglers of Wall Street attempting to use the convention like the wooden figures in a Punch and Judy show.

If they can succeed in deceiving the delegates who have come here under the impression that the Democratic party is expected to make an honest fight against the Republican party, it will be the miracle of modern times.

V

ALTON B. PARKER MADE TEMPORARY CHAIRMAN

Mr. Bryan's letter in morning newspapers of Wednesday, June 26th.

Baltimore, June 25.—When the subcommittee acted on the temporary chairmanship, we were all anxious to know how the full committee would stand on the question, and when the full committee presented Judge Parker we awaited the action of the convention.

Our curiosity is now satisfied. We know what kind of a convention we have and henceforth we can watch its developments with the assurance that nothing will be done that has not the O. K. of Tammany's boss, and that he will not give his approval to anything until it has been submitted to Thomas Fortune Ryan for his consent.

Unless these delegates hear from home and are frightened out of the plans which they now have in mind the platform will be disappointing and its nominee will be a reactionary or a conservative who is satisfactory to the reactionaries.

There could be no mistake about the vote this afternoon. While the majority for Judge Parker was not as large as the polls brought in to me in the forenoon indicated it would be, it was large enough for all practical purposes—the vote for Judge Parker was 579 to 510 for me. It is safe to say that I did not have the vote of a single reactionary, and, unless I have some better evidence than has been expressed, I shall not believe that I lost the vote of a single progressive.

Of course there were progressives whose votes were cast for Judge Parker under the unit rule, and these should not be classed with the reactionaries, but I do not know of any ground upon which a progressive could have voted against me, unless it were a personal ground, and it would be an unfair reflection upon the patriotism of any man to say that he would allow hostility to an individual to influence his vote on a question where a principle was involved.

Possibly account should be taken of another influence, viz.: the interest or the supposed interest of candidates. Mr. Underwood asked the Alabama delegation to vote for Parker. I do not know whether similar requests were sent to Mississippi, Georgia and Florida or not, but Mississippi and Georgia voted solidly for Parker, and he also received all but one of Florida's vote.

Mr. Harmon's Ohio vote was cast solidly for

Parker, presumably in his interest, if not at his request. Twelve of the fourteen votes of Connecticut went to Parker, and it is fair to assume that this was agreeable to Gov. Baldwin. North Dakota's ten votes were cast for me, with the approval of Gov. Burke, who announced in advance his opposition to Parker.

Gov. Wilson came out strong against Parker and so far as I know I received all the votes of the Wilson delegates. There may have been exceptions, but if so they have not been brought to my attention.

The Clark vote was divided. A number of the western states instructed for Clark cast their votes for me. Washington, Idaho, Wyoming, Kansas, half of Colorado, and half of Iowa were some of the Clark delegations that voted against Parker. In the Oklahoma delegation the Wilson half voted for me and the Clark half for Parker. Missouri gave the largest share of her votes to Parker.

It was understood that Mr. Clark himself was not taking sides, but his managers worked manfully for Parker. Mr. Bell of California, one of the leaders in the Clark campaign, took the floor in favor of Judge Parker. Senator Stone and ex-Senator Du Bois were among the most enthusiastic of the Parker supporters.

Kentucky, a Clark state, went so far as to instruct its committeemen to vote for Parker as

CONVENTION STUDIES.
(*Rollins Kirby in "Collier's Weekly." Reproduced by Permission.*)

against James, who was first put forward as Mr. Clark's choice, and who received twenty votes in the full committee.

As Mr. Clark expressed his willingness to allow each of his supporters to follow his own judgment in this contest, it is evident that there are quite a number of men instructed for Clark who have no sympathy with progressive ideas—men who if they are ever released from the support of Mr. Clark may be expected to take up with a reactionary. This is an element that must be taken into account in making calculations upon the ticket that is to be nominated. The lineup to-day is therefore important. It is also important in that it enables the folks at home to know what their representatives are doing at Baltimore.

A word as to the fight over temporary chairman. I several weeks ago advised the committee to insure harmony by selecting a chairman acceptable to Clark and Wilson, they together having more than half of the convention, if not two-thirds. As both have been running as progressives and the chief effort on the part of the friends of each being to prove him a better progressive than the other, I thought there would be no difficulty in securing an agreement in regard to a chairman, and this agreement would have insured the chairman's acceptance without a contest.

The committee, however, brought out Parker and

pitted him against Congressman Henry, the choice of Mr. Wilson, and Congressman James, the choice of Mr. Clark. When the matter went before the full committee the Wilson men, on Gov. Wilson's advice, threw their strength to James, but James could not hold all of the Clark men. I tried to persuade Mr. James to allow the use of his name in the convention contest against Parker, but as Mr. Clark's managers were supporting Judge Parker, even to the extent of having Kentucky's national committeeman vote for Parker—the Kentucky delegation was also largely for Parker—Mr. James did not feel at liberty to enter the contest. I then asked Senator O'Gorman to allow the use of his name, but he felt it his duty to decline.

I then presented the matter to Senator Kern, who was loath to undertake the contest, owing to conditions in his state. However, he agreed last evening to take the matter under consideration. I did not see him any more until after the chairmanship fight was over, but I heard late last night that he had devised a scheme in the interest of harmony which I was glad to approve.

I think the reader, when he has fully digested this scheme, will admit that it is about as good an illustration as has been seen in many a day of the manner in which tact and patriotism can be combined. After I had put Senator Kern in nomination against Parker, he took the platform and made a most forcible and eloquent plea for harmony in the convention.

He called attention to the great issues involved and to the importance of presenting a united front. He then presented a list of names, including Senators O'Gorman, Culberson, Shively and Lea, ex-Gov. Campbell of Ohio, ex-Gov. Folk of Missouri and Representative Clayton of Alabama. He called upon Parker, who sat just in front of him, to join him in withdrawing in favor of any one of these men in order that the convention might open without discord.

It was a dramatic moment. Such an opportunity seldom comes to a man. If Parker had accepted it, it would have made him the hero of the convention. There was a stir in his neighborhood in a moment. The bosses flocked around him, and the convention looked on in breathless anxiety, but he did not withdraw. The opportunity passed unimproved.

Senator Kern then appealed to Mr. Murphy to induce Judge Parker to withdraw, but Mr. Murphy was not in a compromising mood. This was the only thing that Senator Kern did, the good faith f which could be questioned. I am afraid that he ad no great expectation of melting the stony heart of the Tammany boss.

At any rate, nothing came of the generous offer made by Mr. Kern, except that it shifted to the shoulders of Judge Parker and his supporters entire responsibility for any discord that might grow out of the contest.

Judge Parker was escorted to the platform after his nomination had been made unanimous and began to deliver his address, but it had such a moving effect upon the audience that the reading was suspended and the convention adjourned until 8 o'clock this evening.

Various explanations might be given of the actions of the crowd. Probably the most reasonable is that it was half past 3 and many were hungry. There is another explanation, however, that is worth expressing for consideration.

People will not remain in a large hall unless they know what is being said, and Judge Parker's speech was written in the language of Wall street. Only 200 or 300 of the delegates could understand it, and the committee was so busy oiling the machine that it had neglected to provide an interpreter to translate the speech into the every day language of Democrats.

SPEECH OF MR. BRYAN OPPOSING THE ELECTION OF ALTON B. PARKER AS TEMPORARY CHAIRMAN.

Mr. Chairman and Gentlemen of the Convention: I rise to place in nomination for the office of temporary chairman of this convention Hon. John W. Kern of Indiana. In thus dissenting from the judgment of our national committee, as expressed in its recommendation, I recognize that the burden of proof is upon me to overthrow the presumption that the committee is representing the wishes of this convention and of the party of the nation.

I call your attention to the fact that our rules declare that the recommendation of the committee is not final. The very fact that this convention has the right to accept or reject that recommendation is conclusive proof that the presumption in favor of this convention is a higher presumption than that in favor of the wisdom of the committee.

If any of you ask me for my credentials; if any of you inquire why I, a mere delegate to this convention from one of the smaller States, should presume to present a name, and ask you to accept it in place of the name it presented, I beg to tell you, if it needs be told, that in three campaigns I have been the champion of the Democratic party's principles, and that in three campaigns I have received the votes of six millions and a half of Democrats. If that is not proof that I have the confidence of the party of this nation I shall not attempt to furnish proof.

I remind you, also, that confidence reposed in a human being carries with it certain responsibilities, and I would not be worthy of the confidence and the affection that have been showered upon me by the Democrats of this nation if I were not willing to risk humiliation in their defense.

I recognize that a man can not carry on a political warfare in defense of the mass of the people for sixteen years without making enemies; I knew full well that there has been no day since the day I was nominated in Chicago when these enemies have not been industrious in their efforts to attack me from every standpoint.

The fact that I have lived is proof that I have not deserted the people. If for a moment I had forgotten them they would not have remembered me.

I take for my text the quotation that someone has been kind enough to place upon the walls for my use, "He never sold the truth to serve the hour." That is the language of the hero of New Orleans, and I would not deserve the report I have received if I were willing to sell the truth to serve the present hour.

We are told by those who support the committee's recommendation that it is disturbing harmony to oppose their conclusions. Let me free myself from any criticism that any one may have made heretofore or may attempt hereafter. Is there any delegate in this body of more than ten hundred who tried earlier than I to secure harmony in this convention?

I began several weeks ago. I announced to the subcommittee that I would not be a candidate for temporary chairman.

I might have asked, without presumption, that at the end of sixteen years of battle when I find the things I have fought for not only triumphant in my own party but even in the Republican party—under these conditions I might have asked, I repeat, the modest honor of standing before this convention and voicing the rejoicing of my party. But I was more interested in harmony than I was in speaking to the convention. Not only that, but I advised this committee to consult the two leading candidates, the men who together have nearly two-thirds of this convention instructed for them—I asked the committee to consult these two men and get their approval of a man for chairman that there might be no contest in this convention.

What suggestion could I have then made more in the interest of harmony than to ask this committee to allow two-thirds of this convention a voice in the selection of its temporary chairman?

In the discussion before the subcommittee, the friends of Mr. Clark and Mr. Wilson were not able to agree; one supported Mr. James and the other supported Mr. Henry, but in the full committee last night the friends of Mr. Wilson joined with the friends of Mr. Clark in the support of Mr. James, Mr. Clark's choice, and yet the committee turned down the joint request thus made.

I submit to you that the plan that I presented—the plan that I followed—was a plan for securing harmony; and that the plan which the committee followed was not designed to secure harmony.

Let me for a moment present the qualifications of one fitted for this position. This is no ordinary occasion. This is an epoch-making convention. We have had such a struggle as was never seen in politics before. I have been in the center of this fight and I know something of the courage that it has brought forth, and something of the sacrifice that has been required.

I know men working upon the railroad for small wages with but little laid up for their declining years who have disobeyed the railroad managers and helped us in this progressive fight at the risk of having their bread and butter taken from them.

I know men engaged in business and carrying loans at banks who have been threatened with bankruptcy if they did not sell their citizenship, and yet I have seen these men defy those who threatened them and walk up and vote on the side of the struggling masses against predatory wealth.

I have seen lawyers risking their future, by alienating men of large business, in order to be the champions of the poor. I have seen men who had never made a speech before go out and devote weeks of time to public speaking because their hearts were stirred.

It is only fair that now, when the hour of triumph has come, the song of victory should be sung by one whose heart has been in the fight. John W. Kern has been faithful every day in these sixteen years. It has cost him time, it has cost him money, and it has cost him the wear of body and of mind. He has been giving freely of all that he had. Four years ago, when the foundation was laid for the present victory, it was John

W. Kern who stood with me and helped to bring into the campaign the idea of publicity before the election that has now swept the country until even the Republican party was compelled by public opinion to give it unanimous indorsement only a few weeks ago.

It was John W. Kern who stood with me on that Denver platform that demanded the election of senators by direct vote of the people, when a Republican National convention had turned it down by a vote of seven to one, and now he is in the United States Senate, where he is measuring up to the high expectations of a great party.

He helped in the fight for the amendment authorizing an income tax, and he has lived to see a president who was opposed to us take that plank out of our platform and put it through the Senate and House and to see thirty-four states of the union ratify it. And now he is leading the fight in the United States Senate to purge that body of Senator Lorimer, who typifies the supremacy of corruption in politics.

What better man could we have to open a convention?

What better man could we have to represent the spirit of progressive democracy?

Contrast the candidate presented by the committee with the candidate whom I present, and it can be done without impeaching his character or his good intent. Not every one of high character and good intent is a fit man to sound the keynote of a progressive campaign.

There are seven millions of Republicans in this country, or were at the last election, and I have never doubted that a large majority of them were men of high character and good intent, but we would not invite one of them to be temporary chairman of our convention. We have a great many Democrats who vote the ticket after it is nominated, who are not in full sympathy with the purposes of the party.

They emphasize the fact that Judge Parker supported me in 1908, but, I assume that no friend of Judge Parker will contend that he was entirely satisfied with either the candidate or the plans and purposes of our party at that time.

I not only voted the ticket in 1904, but I made speeches for the candidate when I was not at all satisfied with either the candidate or the influences that nominated him and directed the campaign, but the reactionaries did not ask me to act as temporary chairman of the St. Louis convention, altho I had then been twice a candidate for president.

This is not a time when personal ambitions or personal compliments should be considered. We are writing history to-day, and this convention is to announce to the country whether it will take up the challenge thrown down at Chicago by a convention controlled by predatory wealth, or put ourselves under the same control and give the people no party to represent them.

We need not deceive ourselves with the thought that that which is done in a national convention is done in secret.

If every member of this convention entered into an agreement of secrecy we would still act under the eyes of these representatives of the press, who know not only what we do, but why we do it.

The delegates of this convention must not presume upon the ignorance of those who did not come, either because they had not influence enough to be elected delegates or money enough to pay the expenses of the trip, but who have as much interest in the party's welfare as we who speak for them to-day.

These people will know that the influences that dominated the convention at Chicago and made its conclusions a farce are here and more brazenly at work than they were at Chicago.

I appeal to you; let the commencement of this convention be such that the Democrats of this country may raise their heads among their fellows and say: The Democratic party is true to the people. You can not frighten it with your Ryans, nor buy it with your Belmonts.

If the candidate proposed by the committee were an unknown man we would judge him by the forces that are back of him, and not by you, gentlemen, who may try to convince yourselves that you owe it to the committee to sustain its action even tho you believe it made a mistake.

But that is not the question. We know who the candidate is, as well as the men behind him. We know that he is the man who was selected as the party candidate eight years ago when the Democratic party, beaten in two campaigns, decided that it was worth while to try to win a campaign under the leadership of those who had defeated us in the campaigns before.

The Democrats of the country have not forgotten that that convention was influenced by the promise of large campaign funds from Wall street, and they have not forgotten the fact that after corporation management had alienated the rank and file of the party, Wall street threw the party down and elected the Republican candidate.

They have not forgotten that when the vote was counted we had a million and a quarter less votes than we had in the two campaigns before, and a million and a quarter less than we had four years afterward. They have not forgotten that it is the same man, backed by the same influence, who is to be forced on this convention to open a progressive campaign with a paralyzing speech that will dishearten the fighting force of the party.

You ask me how I know, without reading it, that that speech would not be satisfactory. A speech is not so many words; it is the man and not the words that make a speech.

We have been passing through a great educational age; around the world the Democratic movement has been sweeping all obstacles before it. In Russia emancipated serfs have secured the right to a voice in their government. In Persia the people have secured a constitution. In Turkey the man who was in danger every hour of being cast into prison without an indictment, or beheaded without a charge against him, now has some influence in the molding of the laws. China, the sleeping giant of the Orient, has risen from a slumber of two thousand years and to-day is a republic waiting for recognition. And in Great Britain the people have asserted their independence of the House of Lords.

And while the outside world has been marching at double-quick in the direction of more complete freedom our nation has kept step; on no other part of God's footstool has popular government grown more rapidly than here. In every state the fight has been waged. The man whom I present has been the leader of the progressive cause in his state, and once joint leader in the nation.

I challenge you to find in sixteen years where the candidate presented by the committee has, before a nomination was made, gone out and rendered effective service in behalf of any man who was championing the people's cause against plutocracy.

Judge Parker has not been with us; he is not the one to speak to-day.

The Democratic party has led this fight until it has stimulated a host of Republicans to action. I will not say they have acted as they have because we acted first; I will say that at a later hour than we, they caught the spirit of the time and are now willing to trust the people with the control of their own government.

We have been travelling in the wilderness; we now come in sight of the promised land. During all the weary hours of darkness progressive democracy has been the people's pillar of fire by night; I pray you, delegates, now that the dawn has come, do not rob it of its well-earned right to be the people's pillar of cloud by day.

SPEECH OF SENATOR KERN ON THE TEMPORARY CHAIRMANSHIP—A PLEA FOR HARMONY.*

Mr. Chairman and Gentlemen of the Convention—I desire a hearing in order that I may state my reason for not desiring to enter the contest for Temporary Chairman of this convention. I believe that by forty years of service to my party I have earned the right to such a hearing at the hands of a Democratic convention. I hail from the State of Indiana, which will shortly present to this convention for its consideration the name of one of the best, truest, and most gallant Democrats on this earth, in the person of the Hon. Thomas R. Marshall, the Governor of that State.

I desire to take no part in this convention that will in any wise militate against him or against his interests, which all true Indiana Democrats this day loyally support. I have been for many years a personal friend of the gentleman who has been named by the National Committee. Many years ago, when Judge Parker and I were much younger than we are now, we met in a hotel in Europe and became warm personal friends. That was long before his elevation to the Chief Justiceship of the Court of Appeals of his State. Since that time I have enjoyed his friendship. He has had mine. I have accepted the hospitality of his home, and in 1904, when he was a candidate for the Presidential nomination, moved largely by that personal friendship, I enlisted under his standard for the nomination long before the convention, and went through that great battle in St. Louis in his behalf. In that campaign, in response to a request of Judge Parker personally made to me, I, on account of my friendship for him, took the standard of a losing cause as candi-

*After Mr. Bryan had placed Senator Kern in nomination for the temporary chairmanship, Mr. Kern secured recognition and made the speech here printed.

date for Governor of Indiana, and carried it on to defeat, but I hope not an inglorious defeat. In 1908 Judge Parker canvassed in my State for the national ticket, on which I was a candidate for Vice-President. Last year, when I was a candidate for the Senate, in the midst of a heated contest, Judge Parker traveled from New York to Indianapolis to make a speech in my behalf.

We have been during all these years, and are now, personal friends. The greatest desire of my heart is the hope of a Democratic victory. I attended a national convention in Baltimore in 1872, before I had cast a vote, and my young heart was filled with no more enthusiasm for success that year than my old heart is now. I believe Judge Parker is as earnestly in favor, as earnestly desirous of Democratic success this year as I am.

There are only a little over a thousand delegates in this convention; there are seven million Democrats between the oceans. There are millions of Democrats scattered from one end of this Republic to the other who this hour are all looking with aching hearts upon the signs of discord that prevail here when there ought to be forerunners of victory in the shouts of this convention. Is there a man here who does not earnestly desire harmony to the end that there may be victory?

I am going to appeal now and here for that kind of harmony which alone will bring victory. I am going to appeal here and now for that kind of harmony which will change the sadness that this hour exists in millions of Democratic homes into shouts of joy and gladness.

My friend Judge Parker sits before me in this convention, he representing the National Committee, I representing, not another faction, thank God, but representing perhaps another section, and we two men have it in our power to send these words of gladness flashing throughout the Republic. If my friend will join with me now and here in the selection of a man satisfactory to us both; if he will stand in this presence with me and agree that that distinguished New Yorker who has brought more honor to the Empire State in the United States Senate than it has had since the days of Frederick Kernan—James A. O'Gorman—this discord will cease in a moment and the great Democratic party will present a united front. Or if he will agree that that splendid representative from the State of Texas in that same body, Charles A. Culberson, shall preside, or if he will agree upon that splendid parliamentarian, Henry D. Clayton of Alabama, or if he will agree upon that young Tennessean, whose name is known in every home where chivalry abides—Luke Lea—this matter can be settled in a moment. Or if he will agree on the blue-eyed statesman from Ohio, Governor James E. Campbell; or if he will agree on the reform Governor of Missouri, ex-Governor Folk; or if he will agree on my own colleague, the stalwart Democrat from Indiana, Hon. Benjamin F. Shively, all this discord will cease.

Will someone for Judge Parker, will Judge Parker himself, meet me on this ground and aid in the solution of this problem, a solution of which means victory to the party and relief to the taxpayers of the country?

My fellow-Democrats, you will not promote harmony, you will not point the way to victory, by jeering or deriding the name of the man who led your fortunes in 1908. You may put him to the wheel, you may humiliate him here, but in so doing you will bring pain to the hearts of six million men in America who would gladly die for him. You may kill him, but you do not commit homicide when you kill him; you commit suicide.

My friends, I have submitted a proposition to Judge Parker; I submit it to the man, the leader of the New York Democracy, who holds that Democracy in the hollow of his hand. What response have I? [A pause.] If there is to be no response, then let the responsibility rest where it belongs. If Alton B. Parker will come here now and join me in this request for harmony, his will be the most honored of all the names amongst American Democrats.

If there is to be no response, if the responsibility is to rest there, if this is to be a contest between the people and the powers, if it is to be a contest such as has been described, a contest which I pray God may be averted, then the cause to which I belong is so great a cause that I am not fit to be its leader. If my proposition for harmony is to be ignored, and this deplorable battle is to go on, there is only one man fit to lead the hosts of progress, and that is the man who has been at the forefront for sixteen years, the great American tribune, William Jennings Bryan. If you will have nothing else, if that must be the issue, then the leader must be worthy of the cause, and that leader must be William Jennings Bryan.

VI

AN AMAZING SPECTACLE IN THE CONVENTION

Mr. Bryan's letter in afternoon newspapers of Wednesday, June 26th.

Baltimore, June 26.—The smoke of battle has cleared away, and the country is now able to look upon the amazing spectacle of a national convention controlled by a national committee, that committee controlled by a subcommittee of 16, the subcommittee controlled by a group of eight men, these men controlled by Boss Murphy and Boss Murphy controlled by Thomas Fortune Ryan. Probably never before in the history of the country have we seen two men attending a national convention and pulling the strings in the open view of the public. Mr. Ryan, Mr. Belmont and Mr. Morgan have municipal work in New York and Brooklyn that will involve the letting of contracts amounting to more than $250,000,000. This group of financiers also have large financial interests in many of the great cities, and wherever they work they need a political boss.

Some of their bosses work under the name of Democrats and some bear the Republican label, but they all work for their masters. These big financiers have been using the organization of the two leading parties to do their service. They were exposed last week at Chicago, and because of the exposure Mr. Taft's election was made impossible unless they could control the Democratic party and prevent the nomination of a progressive around whom both Democrats and progressive Republicans could rally. I did not believe until I reached Baltimore that it was possible for them to control this convention, but I find that the delegates who know what the interests want and, knowing it, are willing to help the interests, are more numerous than I had supposed.

Many of them came masquerading as progressives and as supporters of progressive candidates. Besides these, who know what they want and know how to get it, there are those who can be deceived with the argument that harmony is more important than principle—an argument always used when the gang gets control of the organization, but never heard when the gang loses control. Then there are some who regard everything from the standpoint of its influence upon the candidate whom they favor. Adding these groups together, they constitute a majority of this Convention, and they have put the party in a false light before the country. The

Democratic party is progressive. Three-fourths, if not nine-tenths of the rank and file have no sympathy whatever with the effort to use the party organization in the interests of a few exploiters, but the masses are temporarily helpless when they are misrepresented by those whom they have elected delegates. The action of the Convention yesterday will open the eyes of the voters at home, and pressure from home may be brought to bear upon the Convention to shake it loose from its alliance with the plunderbund.

If I were a cartoonist, I would represent Ryan as the dominant power in the Convention, having in his hand a cat-o'-nine-tails, the nine tails representing Murphy, Taggart, Sullivan & Co., the dominating members of the national committee, and I would represent the Democratic party as receiving the lashes upon its back. After the people had had a chance to study the cartoon for a while I would draw another representing the party in rebellion against Ryan, snatching the cat-o'-nine-tails from his hand and driving him from power.

That is the situation as I see it. The first thing for the Democratic party to do is to get rid of those members of the national committee who hold the people in contempt and to whom the will of the Money Trust is law. A campaign at such a time as this will be a farce if such men direct it. If the Democratic party has not virtue enough to re-

A Cartoon Drawn from Mr. Bryan's Suggestion.
(*Johnson in the Baltimore "American."*)

"If I were a cartoonist I would represent Ryan as the dominant power in the convention, having in his hand a cat-o'-nine tails, the nine tails representing Murphy, Taggart, Sullivan & Co., the dominating members of the National Committee, and I would represent the Democratic party as receiving the lashes upon its back."—*William Jennings Bryan in his newspaper letter of June 26.*

pudiate this band of buccaneers, now that it has been exposed, it cannot hope to appeal to the confidence of the people. Any candidate for president who enters into collusion with them will find them a millstone about his neck.

I do not believe that they can succeed in nomi-

ANOTHER CARTOON DRAWN FROM THE SUGGESTION MADE BY MR. BRYAN.
(*From the Washington "Times."*)

nating anybody whom they favor, but the nomination will be a mere formality if they do succeed. This is no time for protestations of party loyalty or for the paying of empty compliments. The American people are demanding relief from the despotic power of organized greed. Unless the Democratic party is ready to give them this relief, the Convention might as well adjourn and let the delegates go home by trains that arrive near the middle

CARTOON DRAWN FROM MR. BRYAN'S SUGGESTION FOR A SECOND ONE.
(*From the Washington "Times."*)

"After the people had had a chance to study that cartoon for awhile (the reference is to the cartoon shown on the preceding page), I would draw another representing the party in rebellion against Ryan, snatching the cat-o'-nine-tails from his hand and driving him from power."—*William Jennings Bryan.*

of the night—late enough to avoid the reception committees that will be ready for some of them if they reach home in the daytime.

VII

THE TIDE TURNS

Mr. Bryan's letter in morning newspapers of Thursday, June 27th.

Baltimore, Md., June 26.—To-day has been a day of triumph for the progressives. The men who voted for Judge Parker for chairman have been trying to square themselves. They have been hearing from home. The telegraph companies have been reaping a rich harvest.* No one has suggested that Judge Parker was put up by the telegraph companies for the purpose of increasing their revenues through the protests his nomination would invite, but the money has poured in here just the same.

The effect of these telegrams already is being seen. The resolutions committee wanted a progressive for chairman. I declined the position—although I appreciated the compliment involved

---

* These telegrams were so numerous that an effort was made to ascertain just how many there were. About 110,000 messages are known to have been received by delegates. Some were signed by many persons. Mr. Bryan himself received 1,128 telegrams from 31,331 persons in forty-six States.

in the offer—because I did not want to be hampered by any feeling of obligation to the committee in case I desired to present a minority report. And then, too, I felt that those who owned the ship ought to select the officers to command it.

The committee on permanent organization selected Congressman James, of Kentucky, for permanent chairman. This, however, was not a voluntary offering. A portion of the committee—less than half—attempted to rush the matter through last night and make the temporary organization permanent, but former Gov. Campbell, of Texas, got in just in time to demand an adjournment until morning in order to give all the members a chance to be present.

When the full committee assembled the progressives were out in such force that the effort to continue Parker was abandoned and the honor was given to Mr. James. They then attempted to elect Temporary Secretary Woodson permanent secretary, but this was objected to by the progressives, and Mr. Grattan, of North Carolina, was substituted for him. Thus the progressives had a series of victories.

Before passing from the subject of officers I may add that my refusal of the permanent chairmanship was based partly on the fact that I did not regard it as a compliment to have the position tendered me by those who had defeated me for temporary chairman, and partly because I did not feel disposed to accept any responsibility for the conduct of the convention until it had done something to purge itself of its reactionary character.

As soon as the resolutions committee was organized I introduced a resolution declaring it to be the sense of the committee that the candidates for president should be nominated before the platform was adopted, giving as my reasons that this convention was of unusual importance and that our hope of victory depended upon our measuring up to the requirements of the occasion; that the platform would not amount to much unless our candidate stood squarely upon it and was able to defend it; that a joint debate between our platform and our candidate would be fatal to the prospects of our party, and that by changing the order we would be able so to shape our platform utterances as to give force to his candidacy.

To the argument that it was unprecedented I replied that extraordinary conditions required extraordinary remedies. To the suggestion that any candidate who might be nominated would be willing to stand upon a platform prepared by the convention I replied that our candidate eight years ago amended our platform by telegraph, and that method of amending a platform did not take well with the public. There was considerable discussion, but the sentiment soon turned so strongly to

THE BALTIMORE TRANSFORMATION.
(*Bart in the Minneapolis "Journal."*)

the proposition that it was adopted on roll-call by a vote of 41 to 11.

Senator Vardaman, who was one of the active supporters of the resolution, moved that a committee of three be appointed to notify the committee on rules. The committee on rules, after a short discussion, indorsed the proposition by a vote of 22 to 16, and if it is indorsed by the convention—the convention has not taken action at this hour—the nominations will proceed while the platform is being prepared, and we shall have the benefit of the suggestions of our nominee before putting the finishing touches on the platform.

The air is full of rumors in regard to combinations in behalf of different candidates. One thing is certain—that Gov. Harmon is no longer a possibility. With only nine instructed votes outside of his own State and nineteen delegates from his own State opposing the unit rule, he cannot be considered a factor. The vote yesterday afternoon shows that he cannot secure one-third of the convention under any circumstances.

Mr. Underwood might do a little better than Gov. Harmon, but the triumph of the reactionaries yesterday has so aroused the country that the convention is much less likely to nominate either of these men than it would have been had the machine been willing to allow the convention to begin harmoniously.

However, neither Gov. Harmon nor Mr. Underwood had any chance of nomination before, and they probably thought they had nothing to lose by making the fight that they did for Judge Parker.

Gov. Baldwin's vote is purely complimentary and will not stay with him more than a ballot or two.

Gov. Burke's vote is complimentary also and will go to Gov. Wilson as soon as the former's name is withdrawn.

Gov. Foss' name is not to be presented except in case of a deadlock. Massachusetts' strength, therefore, will be thrown to Clark on the first ballot. I do not feel free to discuss the situation as it relates to Clark and Wilson because I have not expressed a preference between them.

VIII

BOSSISM BECOMES AN ISSUE

Mr. Bryan's letter in afternoon newspapers of Thursday, June 27th.

Baltimore, June 27.—Down with the bosses! That is the supreme duty of this convention. A nomination secured by the aid of these notorious agents of the predatory interests would not be worth having unless it was accepted for the purpose of preventing the Democratic party from defeating Mr. Taft. The object of the Ryan-Murphy-Sullivan-Taggart crowd is not to nominate a Democrat who can win, but to carry out the schemes of the exploiters who work along non-partisan lines and control all parties for their own advantage. The only way in which they can succeed is to pit big business with its trained corps of attorneys and its disciplined crowd of bosses against an unorganized multitude. It is the fight of the wolf against the lamb, but such a fight can only be successful when the people are uninformed. There is a mighty, latent power in the masses which needs only to be brought into action to thwart the wicked schemes of the privileged few.

The masses are now awake. It is doubtful whether we have ever had in this country a better illustration of the moral power of the people than we have had since Tuesday. In the Chicago convention of last week the delegates were outspoken in their support of Taft or in their opposition to him. They were elected on that platform. There were but few changes announced after the delegations reached Chicago, and those who changed were objects of suspicion. When a man deserted his side at Chicago the question was, "What was the price?" For a while it looked as if market quotations might play a part if in the lineup there was a difference of but a few votes. Here it is different. Three-fourths of the delegates to this convention came as progressives; yes, more than three-fourths. There were probably not 150 delegates in the convention who would state in writing that they were not in harmony with the progressive movement.

But since reaching here it has become apparent that many of these men deliberately deceived their constituents. Some protested that they were sustaining the committee in its recommendations out of a desire to promote harmony, although the committee itself was doing everything possible to prevent harmony; others explained their votes by saying that the interests of their candidates demanded it, but the telegraph wires have been busy, and some of the messages are interesting reading. It is noticeable, however, that all the explaining is being done by the followers of Ryan and Murphy. The progressives are being urged to stand firm and make no concessions to the political pirates who are trying to capture the good ship Democracy. Some of the delegates who wandered from the fold and supported the reactionaries are reading telegrams that make their ears burn. One telegram from the West signed by a large number of citizens inquired the name of a delegate who voted for Parker for temporary chairman and suggested that he prepare himself for a lynching on his arrival home. So the war goes merrily on, with the party's hope dependent on the convention's ability to put itself before the country as a true representative of Democracy.

There is one way in which the foul blot can be removed, namely, by a resolution adopted by the convention denouncing any alliance between the money magnates of the country and the party leaders and authorizing the nominee of the party to remove from the national committee any member who has the brand of Wall Street upon him. If the convention will pass such a resolution and then demand of each candidate before voting for him that he will put this resolution in force and reorganize the national committee on a basis of honesty and Democracy, we can win this fight. The country is waiting for a party that dares to defend popular government and the right of each citizen to equal treatment before the law. Mr. Taft can be defeated by 2,000,000 votes if this convention will do its duty. If it fails to do its duty it will not only disappoint millions of Democrats, but it will lose such an opportunity as seldom comes to a party.

IX

THE ANTI-MORGAN-RYAN-BELMONT RESOLUTION

Mr. Bryan's letter in morning newspapers of Friday, June 28th.

Baltimore, Md., June 27.—The day has not been a dull one, notwithstanding the fact that there was little business to do. The afternoon session was devoted to the argument of the South Dakota case. The argument was so complicated that men voted more according to their opinions of its effect than upon the merits of the case.

The Wilson delegates had a plurality at the primaries; this was not denied, but the Clark delegates claimed the right to represent the State on the ground that there were two Clark tickets and that the combined vote for these tickets exceeded the vote for the Wilson ticket.

The trouble was that one of the Clark tickets was headed "Bryan, Wilson, Clark," and it was impossible, therefore, to determine how many of the votes cast were really cast for Clark and how many were influenced by the fact that Wilson's name was combined with Clark's. At least this was the argument of the Wilson men to the claim presented by the Clark men. When the roll was called the Wilson delegation had a considerable majority in its favor.

During the progress of the debate there were demonstrations first for Clark and then for Wilson. At the evening session I introduced the following resolution:

"Resolved, That in this crisis in our party's career and in our country's history this convention sends greeting to the people of the United States and assures them that the party of Jefferson and of Jackson is still the champion of popular government and equality before the law. As proof of our fidelity to the people we hereby declare ourselves opposed to the nomination of any candidate for president who is the representative of or under any obligation to J. Pierpont Morgan, Thomas F. Ryan, August Belmont, or any other member of the privilege-hunting and favor-seeking class."

As introduced, the resolution contained another paragraph, or rather a second resolution, as follows:

"Be it further Resolved, that we demand the withdrawal from this convention of any delegate or delegates constituting or representing the above-named interests."*

The second resolution was attacked more fiercely than the first on the ground that each State had a right to send as its delegates whom it pleased and that to demand the withdrawal of a delegate would be an infringement upon the right of the State. Seeing that this second resolution would be made an excuse by those who did not want to vote for the first resolution I withdrew it before the vote was taken. Then, too, the objection was urged by some with perfect sincerity, and I did not care to put them in a position where their reason for voting "no" would become a matter of discussion.

In a short speech supporting the first or main resolution I called attention to the extraordinary situation and the menace of these influences to our party's success, insisting that we must convince the country that our candidate was free from alliance with the predatory interests.

To the suggestion that such a resolution disturbed the harmony of the party and endangered our candidate I replied with a Bible quotation, "If thy right hand offend thee, cut it off," and con-

* Just as the manuscript of this work was going to the printer the editor ascertained that the introduction of this resolution was first suggested to Mr. Bryan by his brother, Charles W. Bryan, who has been associated with him for several years both in politics and in the publication of "The Commoner."

tended that the same principle that would lead one to cut off his hand to save his body should lead us to free the Democratic party from the influences of these men and those associated with them in schemes of exploitation.

I first asked unanimous consent for the immediate consideration of the resolution. When objection was made I moved to suspend the rules and proceed to the consideration of the motion.

The motion to suspend the rules requires a two-thirds vote for its adoption, and I was afraid that I could not secure a two-thirds vote, but as a majority vote would answer the same purpose—that is, it would become the sense of the convention—I thought it would make no difference whether it received two-thirds or not, and even if it failed to receive a majority it gave a chance to put the delegates on record on the proposition.

The adoption of the resolution by a vote of 889 to 196 eliminates all the reactionaries and narrows the contest down to those about whose progressiveness there can be no doubt.

If the convention puts up a progressive platform and our candidate secures such a reorganization of the national committee as to make that organization worthy of the confidence of the country we can enter upon a winning campaign.

The nominations are now being made to a crowded house and the names of those presented are being cheered by their partisans. It is impossible to make any forecast as to the result. It seems unlikely that a nomination can be made on the first ballot, and as no one can tell how long instructed delegates will regard their instructions as binding or what they will do when they are free to vote as they please, a guess upon the situation is hazardous.

One thing is certain—the convention is more entertaining than was expected. The feeling is not as tense as it was at Chicago and the delegates and visitors seem to be enjoying themselves. I cannot say so much for the dominant element in the national committee.

X

THE ADOPTION OF THE RESOLUTION

Mr. Bryan's letter in afternoon newspapers of Friday, June 28th.

Baltimore, June 28.—It was a surgical operation, and it was possibly a mistake not to have administered chloroform, but I did not expect quite so much tumult. Strange what a consternation can be brought into a political convention by the introduction of a moral issue. If I had offered a resolution declaring that all Republicans are rascals and all Democrats angels, and pledging the Democratic party to give the people a perfect government, Boss Murphy would have seconded the motion. Ryan and Belmont would have shouted themselves hoarse and Flood would have declared that I was as good as a Virginia Democrat. But when I called the country's attention to the fact that we had in the convention two men who are politically sexless, who have no god but money, and who do not hesitate to use political power for their own enrichment, I at once became "a disturber of peace'' and an "enemy of the Democratic party.''

If my conduct was so reprehensible, if my resolution was so offensive, if I was injuring the chances of the Democratic party by introducing it, why did Virginia cast 23½ votes for it and only a half vote against it? If ex-Governor McCorkle represented West Virginia in the speech that he made, why did he not get more than three votes against it in his delegation? If I was jeopardizing the interests of our party why did Florida give three-fourths of her votes to the resolution? Why did poor Alabama have to get out of the trap by changing her vote? She came first on the roll, and, supposing by the speeches made that the resolution was going to be opposed, she started out boldly against it—and after that it snowed. Why did not the New York men who hissed and hooted at the resolution have the courage to vote against it? Shakespeare explains it—"It is conscience that makes cowards of us all.''

Belmont and Ryan have been plowing with our heifer; they have been employing the methods usually resorted to by the predatory interests, and the men whom they were leading astray were protesting that they were just as progressive as anybody. They were insisting that their objection to Mr. Bryan was a personal objection. They were "tired of him, opposed to his dictation," etc. If things had run along smoothly these men would have helped to nominate a gold-plated servant of Wall Street and then gone home to help elect Taft. But things did not run along smoothly, and hence a scene that it would be difficult to describe.

Looking down from the stage I saw a confusion that I never witnessed before in a convention. The delegate section was like a great, boiling spring. Men were shaking their fists at each other, some shouting anathemas at any one who would dare to uncover them, and others clamoring to be counted in favor of the resolution. There is nothing more timid than a politician, except two politicians. The ratio of moral courage in the plain, everyday voter as compared with the courage of the average delegate to a national convention is about 16 to 1. If a national convention could assemble and do its work and then take a recess for a month and allow the final action to be taken after the delegates had returned from a visit home, our conventions would come much nearer representing the people. I would not advise that, however, in the present case, for fear some of the delegates might not be able to get back.

But the convention has done one thing, if nothing else. It has committed a great party more openly to opposition to the Plunderbund than any great party was ever committed before by a national convention.

Political life has both its trials and its rewards. The greatest trial, aside from absence from home and physical strain, is the alienation of friends— not personal, but political. Every new issue brings a new alignment, and men who have associated with others politically find that they must separate. Such separations, however, ought not to affect personal relations. Men should recognize in each other the right to follow conscience and judgment. The more unpleasant separations are those that do not follow a difference of conviction upon some new issue, but are due to a changed environment.

There are several illustrations of it in this convention. Take the case of Bell, of California, for instance. He was my enthusiastic political supporter from 1896 until after 1908—just when the change took place I do not know. I had such confidence in him that I secured his appointment as temporary chairman of the last Democratic national convention. Now I find him so influenced by another environment that he prefers a keynote from Judge Parker, rather than the kind of a speech I am in the habit of making. Has my brand of Democracy changed, or has his? Then there is Urey Woodson. I became acquainted with him 17 years ago, and for many years I had no more loyal supporter. He is now secretary of the national committee, or was until day before yesterday, because I permitted him to be. There were protests against his reappointment four years ago, and I had some misgivings myself, but I gave him the benefit of the doubt. I soon learned of my mistake, but did not think the position important enough to justify a change during the campaign. The gulf has widened between our political views until now my kind of Democracy is quite repulsive to him. Taggart and Sullivan do not owe me anything, unless it be a grudge. I tried to unseat Mr. Sullivan's delegation eight years ago at St. Louis and objected to his reelection as national committeeman four years ago. I was not surprised, therefore, to find him lined up with Wall Street. Taggart is an organization Democrat. It would be hard to get him to bolt a ticket. His loyalty to the party was probably never more severely tested than when I was nominated four years ago. It would not be necessary to recall the fact that he was not reelected chairman of the committee four years ago. The difference in viewpoint would account for his opposition, without recourse to any special grievance.

There are others, but the above illustrate what I mean when I say that politics has its sad side, but there are compensations, and no one knows this better than the writer. The loyalty of friends who fight my battles for me without suggestion from me and without hope or thought of reward; these are like the morning sun; they dispel the darkness.

And what a joy it is to meet these congenial spirits, assembled here from every part of this country! One never appreciates that man is made in the image of his Creator until he comes into contact with a heaven-born soul—a man who is not afraid to die. An ancient proverb says that "no one need be a slave who has learned how to die." The trouble with so many men is that they do not believe in a resurrection. They do not seem to know that Truth cannot die; that no grave can confine it. I saw a lot of brave men at Chicago, fighting for the people. We have a lot of brave men here fighting on the same side. May their tribe increase! *

MR. BRYAN'S SPEECH ON THE RESOLUTION.

Mr. Chairman: I have here a resolution which should, in my judgment, be acted upon before a candidate for president is nominated, and I ask unanimous consent for its immediate consideration.

> "Resolved, That in this crisis in our party's career and in our country's history this convention sends greetings to the people and assures them that the party of Jefferson and Jackson is still the champion of popular government

---

* The above letter has by some been thought to be the best of those written by Mr. Bryan at Chicago and Baltimore. The closing paragraph, written under the stress of stirring events, reveals Mr. Bryan's faith and philosophy in his individual as in his political life.

and equality before the law. As proof of our fidelity to the people we hereby declare ourselves opposed to the nomination of any candidate for President who is a representative of, or under any obligation to J. Pierpont Morgan, Thomas F. Ryan, August Belmont, or any other member of the privilege-hunting and favor-seeking class.

"Be it further resolved, That we demand the withdrawal from this convention of any delegate or delegates constituting or representing the above-named interests."

This is an extraordinary resolution, but extraordinary conditions require extraordinary remedies. We are now engaged in the conduct of a convention that will place before this country the Democratic nominee, and I assume that every delegate in this convention is here because he wants that nominee elected.

It is that we may advance the cause of our candidate that I present this resolution. There are questions of which a court takes judicial notice, and there are subjects upon which we can assume that the American people are informed. There is not a delegate in this convention who does not know that an effort is being made right now to sell the Democratic party into bondage to the predatory interests of this country. It is the most brazen, the most insolent, the most impudent attempt that has been made in the history of American politics to dominate a convention, stifle the honest sentiment of a party and make the nominee the bond-slave of the men who exploit the country.

I need not tell you that J. Pierpont Morgan, Thomas F. Ryan and August Belmont are three of the men who are connected with the great money trust now under investigation, and are despotic in their rule of the business of the country and merciless in their command of their slaves.

Some one has said that we have no right to demand

the withdrawal of delegates who come here from a sovereign State.

I reply that if these men are willing to insult six and a half million of Democrats by coming here we ought to be willing to speak out against them and let them know we resent the insult.

I, for one, am not willing that Thomas F. Ryan and August Belmont shall come here with their paid attorneys and seek secret counsel with the managers of our party. No sense of politeness or courtesy to such men will keep me from protecting my party from the disgrace that they bring upon it.

I can not speak for you. You have your own responsibility, but if this is to be a convention run by these men; if our nominee is to be their representative and tool, I pray you to give us, who represent constituencies that do not want this, a chance to go on record with our protest against it. If any of you are willing to nominate a candidate who represents these men or who is under obligation to these men, do it and take the responsibility. I refuse to take that responsibility.

Some have said that we have no right to demand the withdrawal of delegates from this convention. I will make you a proposition. One of these men sits with New York and the other with Virginia. If the State of New York will take a poll of its delegates and a majority of them—not Mr. Murphy, but a majority of the delegates—I repeat, if New York will on roll-call where her delegates can have their names recorded and printed, ask for the withdrawal of the name of Mr. Belmont; and if Virginia will on roll-call ask the withdrawal of the name of Mr. Ryan, I will then withdraw the latter part of the resolution, which demands the withdrawal of these men from the convention. I will withdraw the last part at the request of the States in which these gentlemen sit, but I will not withdraw the first part that demands that our candidate shall be free from alliance with them.

It is not necessary for the gentleman from Virginia

to deliver a eulogy upon his State. My father was born in Virginia and no one has greater reverence for that great commonwealth than I. I know, too, the sentiment of the people of Virginia. They have not only supported me in three campaigns, but in the last campaign they refused to allow their leading men to go to the convention except under instructions to vote for my nomination. Neither is it necessary for me to defend my reputation as a Democrat. My reputation would not be worth defending if it were necessary to defend it against a charge made against me by any friend of Thomas F. Ryan.

The resolution is not only sober and serious, but it is necessary. We plant ourselves upon the Bible doctrine, "If thy right hand offend thee, cut it off." The party needs to cut off those corrupting influences to save itself.*

THE CANDIDATES DISCUSSED

(A Statement to the Press on Sunday Evening, June 30, by Mr. Bryan, and Given Here as It Appeared in The Chicago "Tribune.")

"I see no reason why we should not conclude the convention with the nomination of both a President and

---

* Before the vote was taken Mr. Bryan withdrew the latter part of his resolution in order that honest friends might not be embarrassed by the argument that the demand for withdrawal of the offending delegates invaded the rights of the State, and in order that the second part of the resolution might not be used as an excuse by those who desired to vote against the main resolution.

When the latter part was withdrawn, the first resolution, pledging the party not to nominate a candidate who was a representative of, or under obligation to, Morgan, Ryan, Belmont, or any other member of the privilege-hunting and favor-seeking class, was adopted by a vote of 889 to 196.

a Vice-president. The friends of the various candidates have fought out their differences, and in their loyalty to the men of their choice have consumed more time than is usually devoted to balloting. There is every reason why the progressives should get together and select a ticket."

Mr. Bryan said he took it for granted there was no chance for the nomination of either Harmon of Ohio, or Underwood of Alabama, whom he designated as the choice of a reactionary element in the party.

He suggested that if the convention could not agree upon either Gov. Wilson of New Jersey or Speaker Clark of Missouri, an available man to head the ticket might be found in a list which he furnished, comprising the names of Senator Kern of Indiana, Senator Elect Ollie James of Kentucky, Senator O'Gorman of New York, Senator Culberson of Texas, and Senator Rayner of Maryland. Continuing, Mr. Bryan said:

"The antagonisms which have been aroused during the preliminary campaign—antagonisms which ought not to have been aroused—should not prevent the coming together of delegates upon some common ground.

"New York is not necessary to a nomination, and under the circumstances should not be permitted to dictate the nomination. I do not mean to say that the vote of New York would vitiate the nomination if the candidate had enough votes to nominate him without New York, for in that case the party would not be under obligation to Mr. Murphy for his nomination; but if Mr. Murphy furnishes the votes necessary to carry the candidate across the line, the candidate who accepts the nomination under those circumstances puts himself under obligations to Mr. Murphy and to the influences which speak through and control him.

"I contend that a candidate so obligated would not appeal to the confidence of the public and would not, if successful at the election, be free to serve the public with singleness of purpose.

"There is not an aspirant for the nomination who would have dared to go out before the people of any State and say: 'I have the promise of Charles F. Murphy that he will deliver to me ninety votes which, under the unit rule, are in his control as soon as I have enough more to give me the necessary two-thirds.'

"I believe, therefore, that all progressives are justified in refusing support to any candidate who desires the New York support and justified in withdrawing support if, after giving it, New York should seek to add enough votes to give the candidate the nomination.

"We have any number of available men from whom to make the selection; a number of them are participating in this convention, and some are candidates before it.

"If either Mr. Clark or Mr. Wilson will announce his willingness to rely entirely upon the progressive vote and his determination not to accept the nomination, if given under conditions which would obligate him to Mr. Murphy, there is no reason why the convention should not agree on one of these.

"If the feeling that has been aroused between the two leading candidates is such that the progressive forces cannot agree upon either, it ought to be easy to agree upon some third person who, not having been a candidate, is not handicapped by animosities engendered or by an adverse verdict at the Democratic conventions and primaries.

"I will not discuss the relative merits of the candidates now before the convention who can be counted as progressive, and I take it for granted that there is now no possibility of the nomination of the two candidates, Gov. Harmon and Mr. Underwood, who were the choice of the reactionaries.

"I do not mean to be understood as saying that all who favor them are reactionaries, but where the two candidates had strength outside of their own localities the support is to be explained, as a rule, by the reactionary tendencies of the supporters.

"We have several persons taking part in this convention, who have not been placed in nomination, who are entirely worthy of consideration.

"Senator Kern of Indiana already has received the support of nearly six millions and a half of Democrats for the vice presidency, and since that time he not only has been elected to the United States senate, but has distinguished himself among his associates by the prominent part he has taken. He is the leader in the fight against Senator Lorimer.

"If there can be no agreement upon one of those now being balloted for it ought to be easy to compromise on a man like Senator Kern.

"Congressman James, our permanent chairman, is a national character, one of the leaders of the house of representatives, and a progressive who has been in the forefront of the fight since 1896.

"Senator O'Gorman, New York's member of the committee on resolutions, is a progressive who has given to his state a distinction of which it has been sadly in need—he has combined a high order of intelligence and courage with a sympathetic devotion to the rights and interests of the common people.

"In addition to those we have Senator Culberson of Texas, a man whose public record would commend him to the progressives of all parties; and I would add Senator Raynor of Maryland, after hearing his strong plea before the resolution in favor of a progressive platform. These are only a few of the names that might be suggested. Surely, with such a wealth of presidential timber we should have no difficulty in nominating a winning ticket.

"Just a word in regard to the vice-presidency. This office should not be regarded lightly nor should the selection be made carelessly. No man is fit to be the vice-presidential nominee who is not equally worthy to be the nominee for president.

"The vice-president should be selected from those available for the presidency, and he should be in harmony with the presidential candidate on all public questions on the fundamental principles which determine the bias and tendencies of men.

"In submitting these views I recognize that I speak merely as an individual, but I am not less interested than the candidates themselves in the nomination of a winning ticket and in the prosecution of a successful campaign, and we shall disappoint those who sent us here if we fail to measure up to the occasion."

XI

AWAITING THE NOMINATION

Mr. Bryan's letter in morning newspapers of Saturday, June 29th.

Baltimore, June 28.—I am writing this report before a nomination is made and cannot, therefore, discuss the candidate. The ballots have not resulted in as many changes as were expected. Rumors have been rife as to what this delegation or that delegation was going to do.

Most attention, of course, is given to New York, because of its large vote, controlled under the unit rule by Murphy. It was reported that New York would vote on the first ballot for Harmon, and on the following ballots for different candidates, but so far Harmon has been the only one to receive the vote. This in itself would ruin Harmon's chances if he were otherwise available. The old doctrine that a man is known by the company he keeps applies in politics as well as elsewhere.

Murphy is in absolute control of the delegation, he is the keeper of New York's conscience—God save the mark! Now the line has been drawn between the sheep and the goats, and New York, in spite of its effort to disguise itself, is among the goats.

When I offered to withdraw the second resolution—the one demanding that Belmont and Ryan leave the convention—New York not only refused to make the request, but demanded a vote on that resolution. I saw that Murphy and his cohorts were looking for an excuse to vote against the resolution and it was partly to deprive them of any excuse that I withdrew the resolution, even without their request.

In connection with this matter I may add that the "sovereign State" argument is sometimes overdone. At Denver four years ago Col. Guffey, of Pennsylvania, marched down the aisle and inquired whether the convention would disregard the action of a sovereign State and throw him out, and the convention said "Yes!" with an emphasis that shook the rafters.

He went back to Pennsylvania and in stentorian tones repeated the question. This time about 400,000 Pennsylvania Democrats trampled on him and stamped around until they nearly caved in the mines. I have not had a chance to consult Col. Guffey, but I am satisfied if he had been a delegate he would have been opposed to interfering with any "sovereign State" provided it would let Wall

Street use it to work its representatives into the convention.

It will be remembered that some of Mr. Lorimer's friends became touchy on the "sovereign State" idea, but the Senate is going to send him back home in spite of the fact that his credentials are regular.

If a national convention has no right to purge itself of such men as Ryan and Belmont, it had better change its rules and secure the right. However, the chastisement which it gave to these two notorious representatives of the interests will probably protect future conventions from a repetition of what has occurred here.

In calculating on the nominee, New York should be counted as a liability rather than as an asset. No Democrat can afford to accept a nomination if New York's vote is necessary to give him two-thirds.

There is no disguising the seriousness of the situation which confronts the Democratic party. It is on trial before the country. It took a long step in advance last night when it had the courage to mention by name three of the most prominent financiers of the country and pledge the nation that its nominee will be free from entangling alliances with them. This resolution is only the beginning. It fixes the standard, but the candidate must measure up to it. The New York delegation is so closely connected with the predatory interests, containing, as it does, trust agents, attorneys and officials, that it would cost a candidate hundreds of thousands of votes to owe his nomination to the delegation.

XII

THE MONEY TRUST'S ACTIVITIES

Mr. Bryan's letter in afternoon newspapers of Saturday, June 29th.

Baltimore, June 29.—We are approaching the climax of this convention. The question that the convention has to decide is whether or not it will live up to the declaration made in the anti-Morgan-Ryan-Belmont resolution. The convention is now pledged by that resolution against the nomination of any man who is a representative of, or under obligation to, Morgan, Ryan, Belmont or any other person representing the favor-seeking and privilege-hunting class.

This is a solemn pledge made to the country. If it is broken it will be broken in the eyes of the public. Before that pledge was made it might have been possible to explain that the candidate was reasonably progressive, because we had no definition of progressiveness to apply to a candidate, but now we have, and if the candidate does not measure up to it the eyes of the public will be fixed upon the space between the candidate's head and the mark that we have drawn on the wall. How can we tell whether a proposed candidate is the representative of, or obligated to, Morgan, Ryan and Belmont, and the interests which they represent? There is just one way, namely, to inquire whether he is willing to accept the nomination at their hands.

It is a principle of law that an election is vitiated by corrupt votes whenever the candidate could not have been elected without these votes, and so a nomination is vitiated when it depends upon votes which are not acceptable under the rules and upon the conditions laid down by this convention in the anti-Morgan-Ryan-Belmont resolution. Mr. Lorimer is about to be expelled from the United States Senate because he accepted a senatorship which depended upon corrupt votes, and the public universally approved the Senate's proposed action. Would the Democratic party approve a nomination made by influences as corrupt as those that secured the Lorimer election?

It is now a matter of public knowledge that the money trust, after controlling the Chicago convention and dictating the Chicago nominee, moved its show to this city, set up its tent and organized a two-ring circus, with all its accessories, from ringmasters down to the red lemonade man. This circus had its acrobats, several of them expert at somersaulting and contortion; it has held sessions in the daytime and at night. Mr. Murphy is general director and resident agent of the concern. He controls the New York delegation under the unit rule as completely as his hand controls his fingers. A candidate who would accept his support would be an ingrate not to repay the obligation in the only coin which is legal tender in the office of the plunderbund, namely, government favors.

Will the Democratic party be democratic? The question is even more fundamental; will it be honest? Will it keep the promise it has made to six million and a half of Democrats and to millions of Republicans? More than 10,000,000 voters are watching the bulletins that come from this convention. Will this convention give these patriotic citizens a leader who will lead?

XIII

HOW VOTES WERE CHANGED

Mr. Bryan's letter in morning newspapers of Monday, July 1st.

Baltimore, June 30.—If I may be permitted to speak of my own part I shall devote a few sentences to the explanation which I gave of the change of twelve of the Nebraska delegates from Clark to Wilson. I was not in the hall Friday night when New York cast its ninety votes for Clark, but went in later during the demonstration.

After having a night to reflect over the matter I decided upon a course of action in case an attempt was made to use the New York vote to elect Mr. Clark. In acting one must always consider the conditions to be met, for conditions are usually the measure of exertion.

At the Chicago convention I saw how unfairly a holdover political machine had made up the temporary roll of the convention and then used the votes of those put upon the roll to seat each other, thus giving to the committee control of the new convention.

I was in a good position to watch the roller as it moved noisily along, overcoming every obstruction, and when its work was completed thwarting the will of a large majority of the Republican party. To add aggravation to the wrong the committee was made up of representatives from the southern States where there is practically no Republican vote.

These committeemen, representing a paper organization and held to the Republican party largely by the power of patronage, were used to outvote the representatives from States that cast a large Republican vote. And to add further cause for indignation this unfairly proportioned committee seated delegates upon the same congressional proportion as in the north.

About the time this outrage on popular governmen had had time to soak in I came to Baltimore and here I found the Democratic national committee acting upon the same plan, using holdover committeemen to misrepresent the delegations, and intending to open a progressive convention with a reactionary keynote.

I soon learned that the same influences which at Chicago defied popular sentiment in the Republican party were here in force. I found that, having defeated the progressive program at Chicago, they were bent upon defeating it here. Here cunning was substituted for boldness, and the progressive brand was being used to mask the real character of the work outlined.

I have already described the first contest in which I was defeated for temporary chairman, a position which I did not desire, and for which I was a candidate only because I felt that some one ought to represent the progressive cause. I have also chronicled the second contest, which resulted in the passage of the Morgan-Ryan-Belmont resolution.

It was the passage of that resolution and the pledge that it gave the public that made it imperative, according to my judgment, that I refuse to enter into partnership with Mr. Murphy in nominating a Democratic candidate.

I felt sure from telegrams received and news reports read that the people were aroused as they had seldom been before to the importance of presenting a candidate upon whose nomination there could be no suspicion of connection with the interests which we had denounced.

It distrest me to have to do anything that might result in injury to the political fortunes of Mr. Clark. I have known him for eighteen years, rejoiced in his selection as minority leader, and a year and a half ago regarded him as more likely than any one else to fit into the conditions in so far as I could then estimate them.

If he had made good use of the opportunity he

THE SACRIFICE HIT.

The Pitcher who has been hit by Mr. Bryan's ball is Charles F. Murphy, of Tammany Hall.

(*Bart in the Minneapolis "Journal."*)

had he would have been nominated by acclamation, but instead of leading the progressive element of the party—the element with which he had always been identified—he became imprest with the idea that his special duty was to harmonize the two elements of the party and prevent any break in the ranks.

The leader and the harmonizer are two entirely different persons, and Mr. Clark chose to be the latter. There are times when the harmonizer is the most available candidate, but the situation is different just now.

The country is alive with progressive ideas and progressivism has not been defeated at Chicago. Two or three million Republicans are following the proceedings of this convention and waiting to see whether they can use the Democratic party for the rebuking of stand-pat Republicanism or be forced to organize a new party.

Mr. Clark's first mistake was in attempting to overlook the radical difference which exists in the Democratic party between the progressives and the reactionaries. His second was in selecting managers who sought to advance his cause by manipulation rather than by that candid appeal which befits the present hour.

After permitting a considerable number of reactionaries to come into the convention under instructions, these managers endeavored to win votes by tying up with the reactionary element of the convention.

While Mr. Clark himself remained neutral in the fight between Judge Parker and myself for temporary chairman, his managers were working like beavers for Judge Parker. They were not even willing for me to take Mr. James, their own candidate, for temporary chairmanship before the subcommittee, and pit him against Parker.

Mr. Clark aroused much hostile criticism when he refused to take sides, and this criticism became more emphatic when New York's vote was welcomed with a great demonstration.

There is too much at stake to risk defeat, as we would risk defeat if we had to spend the campaign in explaining how a candidate could owe his nomination to predatory interests without danger to his administration.

Mr. Clark's friends spurn the thought of his being influenced by such support, but they forget that the mass of the people cannot know Mr. Clark personally, as his intimate friends do.

I know him well enough to have confidence in his high purpose and in his good intent, as I have in the purpose and intent of other candidates. I believe that he would try to carry out the people's will, but few, if indeed any, can entirely fortify themselves against the unscrupulous influence exerted by favors received. We do not allow judges to accept favors from litigants and the President continually acts as an arbiter between the organized and the unorganized masses.

But even if we could feel certain that the securing of a presidential nomination by the aid of those directly connected with the exploiting class would have no influence whatever upon Mr. Clark's official conduct, we could not possibly hope to impart this confidence to millions of voters who, not enjoying the personal acquaintance of Mr. Clark, would have to rely upon newspaper reports, and it must be remembered that in the contested States the Republicans have five to one, if not ten to one, the advantage of us.

I announced that we would withhold our vote from Mr. Clark so long as New York supported him, and that we would apply the same rule to other candidates; that is, that we would not enter into partnership with Wall Street.

MR. BRYAN'S SPEECH EXPLAINING HIS VOTE *

Nebraska is a progressive state. Only twice has she given her vote for a Democratic candidate for President —in 1896 and 1908—and on both occasions her vote was cast for a progressive ticket running upon a progressive platform. Between these two elections, in the elec-

When Nebraska was called on the fourteenth ballot a poll was demanded, and Mr. Bryan in changing his vote made this speech. It marked the turning point in the convention.

tion of 1904, she gave a Republican plurality of 85,000 against a Democratic reactionary. In the recent primary the total vote cast for Clark and Wilson was over 34,000 and the vote cast for Harmon something over 12,000, showing that the party is now nearly three-fourths progressive.

The Republican party of Nebraska is progressive in about the same proportion, and the situation in Nebraska is not materially different from the situation throughout the country west of the Alleghanies. In the recent Republican primaries, fully two-thirds of the Republican vote was cast for candidates representing progressive policies.

In this convention the progressive sentiment is overwhelming. Every candidate has proclaimed himself a progressive—no candidate would have any considerable following in this convention if he admitted himself out of harmony with progressive ideas. By your resolution, adopted night before last, you, by a vote of more than four to one, pledged the country that you would nominate for the presidency no man who represented, or was obligated to Morgan, Ryan, Belmont, or any other member of the privilege-seeking, favor-hunting class. This pledge, if kept, will have more influence on the result of the election than the platform or the name of the candidate. How can that pledge be made effective? There is but one way, namely, to nominate a candidate who is under no obligation to those whom these influences directly or indirectly control. The vote of the State of New York in this convention, as cast under the unit rule, does not represent the intelligence, the virtue, the democracy or the patriotism of the ninety men who are here. It represents the will of one man—Charles F. Murphy—and he represents the influences that dominated the Republican convention at Chicago and are trying to dominate this convention. If we nominate a candidate under conditions that enable these influences to say to our candidate, "Remember, now, thy creator," we can not hope to appeal to the confidence of the progressive Democrats and Republicans of the nation.

Nebraska, or that portion of the delegation for which I am authorized to speak, is not willing to participate in the nomination of any man who is willing to violate the resolution adopted by this convention and accept the high honor of the presidential nomination at the hands of Mr. Murphy. When we were instructed for Mr. Clark, the Democratic voters who instructed us did so with the distinct understanding that Mr. Clark stood for progressive democracy. Mr. Clark's representatives appealed for support on no other ground. They contended that Mr. Clark was more progressive than Mr. Wilson, and indignantly denied that there was any cooperation between Mr. Clark and the reactionary element of the party. Upon no other condition could Mr. Clark have received a plurality of the Democratic vote of Nebraska.

The delegates for whom I speak stand ready to carry out the instructions given, in the spirit in which they were given and upon the conditions under which they were given; but these delegates will not participate in the nomination of any man whose nomination depends upon the vote of the New York delegation. Speaking for myself and those who join me, we, therefore, withhold our vote from Mr. Clark as long as New York's vote is recorded for him, and I hereby notify the chairman and this convention that I desire recognition to withdraw these votes from any candidates to whom New York's votes are thrown. The position that we take in regard to Mr. Clark we will take in regard to any other candidate whose name is now or may be before the convention. We shall not be parties to the nomination of any man, no matter who he may be or from what section of the country he comes, who will not, when elected, be absolutely free to carry out the anti-Morgan-Ryan-Belmont resolution and make his administration reflect the wishes and hopes of those who believe in a government of the people, by the people, and for the people.

If we nominate a candidate who is under no obligation to these interests, which speak through Mr. Murphy, I shall offer a resolution authorizing and directing the presidential candidate to select a campaign committee to manage the campaign, in order that he may not be compelled to suffer the humiliation or act under the embarrassment that I have in having men participate in the management of his campaign who have no sympathy with the party's aims and in whose democracy the general public has no confidence. At the conclusion of Mr. Bryan's statement ex-Governor McCorkle, of West Virginia, obtained recognition, and, with Mr. Bryan's consent, submitted the following question:

"Are we to understand from what you have said that you will not support the nominee of this convention if he is named by a majority made up in part of the vote of New York?" Mr. Bryan: I shall be pleased to answer the gentleman's question and before answering, will add that if any other gentleman in the convention has a question to ask I shall remain here and give him a chance to ask it. This is a Democratic convention; we have a right to ask questions and we should be frank with each other.

Answering the gentleman from West Virginia, I would reply that nothing that I have said this morning and nothing that I have ever said heretofore justifies the construction which the gentleman would place upon my language. I distinguish between refusing to participate in the nomination of a candidate and refusing to support a candidate nominated over my protest. I distinguish between these two propositions just as the law distinguishes between the act of a lawyer who defends a prisoner after a crime has been committed and the act of a lawyer who conspires with the prisoner to commit a crime. Governor Brewer of Mississippi then obtained recognition, and, with Mr. Bryan's consent, submitted the following queston:

"If Mr. Clark, Mr. Underwood, Mr. Wilson, Mr. Marshall, Mr. Harmon, Mr. Kern, or Mr. Foss is nominated by this convention by a two-thirds majority, with New York voting for the man who is nominated, will you support the Democratic nominee?" Mr. Bryan: I deny the right of any man to put a hypothetical question to me unless he is prepared to include in that question every essential element that enters into it so that the question can be fully understood and intelligently answered.

Having denied the right of the gentleman to ask the question and having called his attention to the fact that he is taking advantage of a political assembly to ask a question which he would not dare to ask in any court of justice I now answer him:

I expect to support the nominee of this convention. I expect the nominee of this convention to be worthy of the support of every delegate. I have no reason to believe that any man will be nominated who would accept a nomination at the hands of Mr. Murphy and the influences back of him. I will not give bond to make further answer to the hypothetical question put by the gentleman from Mississippi until we are in a position to supply the necessary facts which his question omits—facts necessary to an understanding of the situation upon which we will be called to act.

Now, I am prepared to announce my vote, with the understanding that I stand ready to withdraw my vote from the candidate for whom I now cast it if Mr. Murphy casts the ninety votes of New York for him. I cast my vote for Nebraska's second choice—Governor Wilson.*

* On July 30, the Nebraska Democratic State Convention endorsed Mr. Bryan's course at Baltimore by a vote of 636 to 246.

XIV

THE CLOSE OF THE CONVENTION

Mr. Bryan's letter in morning newspapers of Wednesday, July 3d.

Baltimore, July 2.—Although the nomination for vice-president has not yet been made, enough has been done to enable the public to judge the far-reaching effect of this remarkable convention.

Mr. Wilson's nomination is evidently very acceptable to the country. His campaign was a national one from the start. In fact, he was the only candidate who ran everywhere. This had both its advantages and its disadvantages. It was an advantage in that it gave him a chance to secure a larger number of delegates, but it was a disadvantage in that it naturally arrayed against him the friends of the other candidates. He entered the convention, however, with more than 200 votes less than half.

His greatest asset was the fact that he came out strongly against Parker for temporary chairman. This was the first line drawn in the convention, and it was probably fortunate for Wilson that his side was defeated. If I had been selected for temporary chairman it would have been looked upon as a thing to be expected, and a victory at that time would not have made any great impression on the country. But my defeat startled the Democrats throughout the land and made them aware of the strength of the reactionaries.

Hearing from home has been one of the prominent features of this convention. Probably no other convention ever brought forth such a flood of telegrams, and these telegrams had a great deal to do with the final action of the convention. Wilson's name was in nearly all of them.

The weak point in Wilson's campaign for the nomination was the fact that some of his former utterances were used against him by his opponents, but these arguments will not avail when addressed to the progressive Republicans. I think Wilson will poll more of the progressive Republican vote than any other man we could have named.

The platform is progressive, the most progressive platform that any great party has offered to the public. With a vice-president in harmony with the platform and the presidential candidate, we ought to make a great fight and a successful fight. Our party has given the progressives of the nation a rallying and a battle line. Never before has the issue been so clearly drawn between the people on the one side and the predatory interests.

on the other. The resolution naming the leaders of the financial world who have stood behind the great favor-seeking combination was a stroke of policy as well as a triumph of principle.

The one sad feature is the failure of the defeated candidates to realize their ambitions. This failure, of course, did not bring any great disappointment to the candidates who had a small following; their only hope was in the turning up of something unexpected. In the case of Mr. Clark, however, there was reasonable ground for hope, and therefore great disappointment.

There is no boasting of victory among those of his opponents who knew him personally. He is universally beloved and his defeat was not a reflection upon his official record or upon his general merits.

The action of the Republican convention made it necessary that the party should be even more distinctly and outspokenly progressive than it need to have been if Mr. Roosevelt had been nominated —although it could not have retreated from its advanced position in any case.

This convention, too, laid unexpected emphasis upon progressive ideas—a sort of reaction from its first mistake in having the keynote sounded by a reactionary. The resolution against Morgan, Ryan and Belmont raised the expectations of the country and nothing would have satisfied the party but a clear-cut declaration in favor of all needed remedial legislation and a candidate who would be accepted as a fulfilment of the pledge given.

Mr. Clark's managers did not seem to catch the spirit of the occasion, and were guilty of one mistake after another, until their candidate was put in a position where the convention felt that he did not fit into the requirements of the occasion as nearly as Gov. Wilson.

It is too early for me to measure the influence of my own part in the convention, as in every great contest there has been a realignment, and I find some friends alienated and some opponents converted into friends. What a pity that one cannot have the same set of friends and enemies through life. It is so hard to part with those who go from you, and it takes time to get acquainted with those who come to you.

When I left Nebraska I expected to play a minor part in the convention. I had urged the committee to consult Mr. Wilson and Mr. Clark in regard to the chairman, and supposed the convention would be opened without friction.

Knowing the managers for the various candidates would be in charge of the program, I thought it might not be necessary for me to appear upon the floor until after the candidate was nominated. But my plans were overturned and I was forced into a fight at the very outset, in an effort to prevent the opening of the convention on a reactionary key.

The presence of a great collection of representatives of special interests suggested the anti-Morgan-Ryan-Belmont resolution, and then the demand for a poll in my delegation compelled me to make an explanation of my vote earlier than I had expected. There was no program, each act on my part being the result of an unexpected exigency. I did the best I could, following the line of duty as I saw it, and cannot shrink from the consequences. While I have received a great deal of commendation through telegrams, I have received some criticism, but I expect the criticism to soften when the facts are fully understood.

One encouraging thing is the denunciation I have received at the hands of Mr. Hearst. His attacks are so much like the attacks which he made upon me in 1908, when he lent his assistance to Mr. Taft, that I feel that he raises a presumption in my favor, for the platform in 1908 laid the foundation for the victory which has been won in this convention and which I believe will be completed at the polls in November.

MR. BRYAN'S "VALEDICTORY" *

Mr. Chairman and members of the convention: You have been so generous with me in the allowance of time that I had not expected to trespass upon your patience again, but the compliment that has been paid me by the gentleman from the District of Columbia justifies, I hope, a word in the form of a valedictory.

For sixteen years I have been a fighting man. Performing what I regarded as a public duty I have not

---

* The Pittsburgh "Press," describing this incident of the convention, said:

"The voluntary passing of Bryan was the one great dramatic incident of the night. The convention had stopt in the middle of the roll-call to spend a couple of hours disposing of the platform, and the usual resolutions. It was long past midnight when it resumed its labors. The roll was proceeding slowly. The vast auditorium was still jammed with people. The galleries had been listening in amusement to the efforts of orators to pay eloquent tributes to the men they were placing in nomination for the vice-presidency. The heat and the lateness of the hour had had their effect, and 50 per cent. of the crowd was lazily lolling back in chairs, hoping for something to enliven the monotony.

"The reading clerk finally reached the District of Columbia, which was next to the last on the list. He had to call twice. Finally the figure of a fat man climbed on a chair wet with perspiration. His collar was a rag and his general appearance one of complete physical exhaustion. There had been a general laugh from the gallery when this representative of the District, in a voice that penetrated to every part of the big armory, rose to nominate Mr. Bryan for vice-president. The pause which ensued seemed to last ten minutes. It actually lasted ten seconds, and then came the wildest, most hysterical outburst of cheering that had marked the convention. From the delegates themselves, from the galleries, and from the dim recesses of the great dust-filled building there went up a roar that seemed like the whistle of a thousand locomotives merged into one.

"Down in the very front in the seat set apart for him

feared to speak out on every public question before the people of the nation for settlement, and I have not hesitated to arouse the hostility of individuals where I felt it my duty to do so in behalf of my country.

I have never advocated a man except with gladness and I have never opposed a man except in sadness. If I have any enemies in this country, those who are my enemies have a monopoly of hatred. There is not one single human being for whom I feel ill-will. Nor is there one American citizen in my own party or in any other whom I would oppose for anything unless I believed that in not opposing him I was surrendering the interests of my country, which I hold above any person.

I recognize that a man who fights must carry scars and I decided long before this campaign commenced that I had been in so many battles and had alienated so many persons that my party ought to have the leadership of

by the Nebraska delegation was sitting Bryan. Motionless he remained, his palm-leaf fan clenched in his hand; his hair disheveled; his face ashen white. But as the cheering continued and increased in volume a red blush mantled the Commoner's face and head. 'Bryan! We want Bryan!' echoed and re-echoed from one section of the hall to the other and reverberated back from the ceilings until it was deafening. At last Bryan climbed on his chair. 'Platform! Platform!' the refrain went up, and in obedience to the cry, Bryan slowly mounted to the same spot where, a few days ago, he had denounced to their faces Murphy, Ryan and Belmont.

"Bryan did not speak long, but every word he uttered will ever be remembered by those who heard it. He spoke, in a voice that at times trembled with emotion, of regret that the personal enmities he had engendered during the sixteen years he had been leading democracy, made it necessary for him to relinquish the leadership into their hands.

"The presentation of Mr. Bryan's name was made by a District of Columbia delegate whose identity Mr. Bryan has not yet learned. Thus brought before the convention during its closing hours, Mr. Bryan delivered, extemporaneously, his speech which he called his valedictory."

someone who had not thus offended and who might, therefore, lead with greater hope of victory.

To-night I come with joy to surrender into the hands of the one chosen by this convention a standard which I have carried in three campaigns, and I challenge my enemies to say that it has ever been lowered in the face of the foe. The same belief that led me to prefer another for the presidency rather than to be a candidate myself, leads me to prefer another for the vice presidency.

It is not because the vice presidency is lower in importance than the presidency that I decline. There is no office in this nation so low that I would not accept it if I could serve my country by so doing. But I believe that I can render more service when I have not the embarrassment of a nomination and the suspicion of a selfish interest—more service than I could as a candidate,.but your candidate will not be more active in this campaign that I shall be. My services are at the command of the party. I feel relieved that the burden of leadership is transferred to other shoulders.

All I ask is that, having given us a platform, the most progressive that any party has ever adopted in this nation, and, having given us a candidate, who, I believe, will appeal not only to the Democratic vote but to some three or four million of Republicans who have been alienated by the policies of their party, there is but one thing left, and that is to give us a vice president who is also progressive, so that there will be no joint debate between our candidates.

In conclusion, I second the nomination, not of one man, but of two: Governor Burke, of North Dakota, and Senator Chamberlain, of Oregon.

AN INTERVIEW WITH MR. BRYAN

Following the nomination of Governor Wilson for the presidency, Mr. Bryan gave out the following statement to the newspapers, which was published Wednesday morning, July 3d:

"I feel sure that the action of the convention thus far will appeal to the country. I had no choice among the progressive candidates, but from the first included Governor Wilson in every list I had occasion to make. His action in coming out strongly against Mr. Parker for temporary chairman was the turning point in his campaign. The country is progressive; nearly all of the Democratic party and more than half of the Republican party are progressives.

"The paramount question before this convention was whether we would take sides with the reactionaries, thus encouraging the organization of a third party and giving to this third party the hope of defeating the reactionaries divided. This on the one side and the nomination of a ticket that would so appeal to the people as to make a third party impossible were the issues.

"I am satisfied that with Mr. Wilson running for the presidency on such a platform (and I know what this is) there will be very few progressive Republicans who will not feel justified in supporting the Democratic ticket. If I were to make an estimate, I should say that not less than 2,000,000 majority of the popular vote and enough of the electoral college to constitute an overwhelming majority will be found in the Democratic column in November.

"The action of the convention in adopting the anti-Morgan-Ryan-Belmont resolution has demonstrated that the Democratic party is not only progressive, but bold enough to throw down the gauntlet to the predatory interests.

"It is fortunate that Mr. Wilson's nomination was made without the aid of Mr. Murphy. It is no reflection on the many good Democrats in the delegation to say this. From every standpoint the outlook is hopeful.

"When the Republican convention adjourned it became even more evident that circumstances required some emphatic action on the part of our convention to insure a progressive vote under our banner.

"The incidents of the convention have in a strange way emphasized the progressivism of our party far more than I thought, and the convention has decided with rare unanimity that Governor Wilson fits into the conditions which the Republican convention has helped in creating.

"Knowing the contents of the platform, for I helped in framing it, and feeling sure that the nominee for vice-president will strengthen the ticket, it is needless to say that I am gratified to see our party raising the banner of progressive Democracy and calling to the progressive portions of the nation to join in restoring the government to the hands of the people, that it may in truth be a 'government of the people, for the people, and by the people.' It has been a long convention, but the results are well worth the time."

XV

THE DEMOCRATIC PLATFORM

We, the representatives of the Democratic party of the United States, in national convention assembled, reaffirm our devotion to the principles of Democratic government formulated by Thomas Jefferson and enforced by a long and illustrious line of Democratic presidents.

We declare it to be a fundamental principle of the Democratic party that the federal government, under the constitution, has no right or power to impose or collect tariff duties, except for the purpose of revenue, and we demand that the collection of such taxes shall be limited to the necessities of government, honestly and economically administered.

The high Republican tariff is the principal cause of the unequal distribution of wealth, it is a system of taxation which makes the rich richer and the poor poorer; under its operations the American farmer and laboring man are the chief sufferers; it raises the cost of the necessaries of life to them, but does not protect their product or wages.

The farmer sells largely in free markets and buys almost entirely in the protected markets.

In the most highly protected industries, such as cotton and wool, steel and iron, the wages of the laborers are the lowest paid in any of our industries.

We denounce the Republican pretense on that subject and assert that American wages are established by competitive conditions and not by the tariff.

We favor the immediate downward revision of the existing high and, in many cases, prohibitive tariff duties, insisting that material reductions be speedily made upon the necessaries of life. Articles entering into competition with trust controlled products and articles of American manufacture which are sold abroad more cheaply than at home should be put upon the free list.

We recognize that our system of tariff taxation is intimately connected with the business of the country and we favor the ultimate attainment of the principles we advocate by legislation that will not injure or destroy legitimate industry.

We denounce the action of President Taft in vetoing the bills to reduce the tariff in the cotton, woolen, metals, the chemicals schedules and the farmers' free list bill, all of which were designed to give immediate relief to the masses from the exactions of the trusts.

The Republican party, while promising tariff revision, has shown by its tariff legislation that such revision is not to be in the people's interest and having been faithless to its pledges of 1908 it should no longer enjoy the confidence of the nation. We appeal to the American people to support us in our demand for a tariff for revenue only.

The high cost of living is a serious problem in every American home. The Republican party, in its platform, attempts to escape from responsibility for present conditions by denying that they are due to a protective tariff. We take issue with them on this subject and charge that excessive prices result in a large measure from the high tariff laws enacted and maintained by the Republican party and from trusts and commercial conspiracies fostered and encouraged by such laws, and we assert that no substantial relief can be secured for the people until import duties on the necessaries of life are materially reduced and these criminal conspiracies broken up.

A private monopoly is indefensible and intolerable. We therefore favor the vigorous enforcement of the criminal as well as the civil law against trust and trust officials, and demand the enactment of such additional legislation as may be necessary to make it impossible for a private monopoly to exist in the United States.

We favor the declaration by law of the conditions upon which corporations shall be permitted to engage in interstate trade, including, among others, the prevention of holding companies, of interlocking directors, of stock watering, of discrimination in price, and the control by any one corporation of so large a proportion of any industry as to make it a menace to competitive conditions.

We condemn the action of the Republican administration in compromising with the Standard Oil Company and the Tobacco Trust and its failure to invoke the criminal provisions of the antitrust law against the officers of those corporations after the court had declared that from the undisputed facts in the record they had violated the criminal provisions of the law.

We regret that the Sherman antitrust law has received a judicial construction depriving it of much of its efficacy and we favor the enactment of legislation which will restore the statute the strength of which it has been deprived by such interpretation.

We believe in the preservation and maintenance in their full strength and integrity of the three coordinate branches of the federal government— the executive, the legislative and the judicial— each keeping within its own bounds and not encroaching upon the just powers of either of the others.

Believing that the most efficient results under

our system of government are to be attained by the full exercise by the States of their reserved sovreign powers, we denounce as usurpation the efforts of our opponents to deprive the States of any of the rights reserved to them, and to enlarge and magnify by indirection the powers of the federal government.

We insist upon the full exercise of all the powers of the government, both State and national, to protect the people from injustice at the hands of those who seek to make the government a private asset in business. There is no twilight zone between the nation and the State in which exploiting interests can take refuge from both. It is as necessary that the federal government shall exercise the powers reserved to it, but we insist that federal remedies for the regulation of interstate commerce and for the prevention of private monopoly shall be added to and not substituted for State remedies.

We congratulate the country upon the triumph of two important reforms demanded in the last national platform—namely: the amendment of the federal constitution authorizing an income tax and the amendment providing for the popular election of senators, and we call upon the people of all the States to rally to the support of the pending propositions and secure their ratification.

We note with gratification the unanimous sentiment in favor of publicity before the election of campaign contributions—a measure demanded in our national platform of 1908 and at that time opposed by the Republican party—and we commend the Democratic house of representatives for extending the doctrine of publicity to recommendations, verbal and written, upon which presidential appointments are made, to the ownership and control of newspapers, and to the expenditures made by and in behalf of those who aspire to presidential nominations, and we point for additional justification for this legislation to the enormous expenditures of money in behalf of the President and his predecessor in the recent presidential contest for the Republican nomination for President.

The movement toward more popular government should be promoted through legislation in each State which will permit the expression of the preference of the electors for national candidates at presidential primaries.

We direct that the national committee incorporate in the call for the next nominating convention a requirement that all expressions of preference for presidential candidates shall be given and the selection of delegates and alternates made through a primary election conducted by the party organization in each State where such expression and election are not provided for by State law.

Committeemen who are hereafter to constitute the membership of the Democratic national committee and whose election is not provided for by law, shall be chosen in each State at such primary elections and the service and authority of committeemen, however chosen, shall begin immediately upon the receipt of their credentials.

We pledge the Democratic party to the enactment of a law prohibiting any corporation from contributing to a campaign fund and any individual from contributing any amount above a reasonable maximum.

We favor a single presidential term and to that end urge the adoption of an amendment to the constitution making the President of the United States ineligible for reelection, and we pledge the candidate of this convention to this principle.

At this time, when the Republican party, after a generation of unlimited power in its control of the federal government, is rent into factions, it is opportune to point to the record of accomplishments of the Democratic house of representatives in the sixty-second congress. We indorse its action and we challenge comparison of its record with that of any congress which has been controlled by our opponents.

We call the attention of the patriotic citizens of our country to its record of efficiency, economy and constructive legislation:

It has, among other achievements, revised the rules of the house of representatives so as to give to the representatives of the American people freedom of speech and of action in advocating, proposing and perfecting remedial legislation.

It has passed bills for the relief of the people and the development of our country; it has endeavored to revise the tariff taxes downward in the interest of the consuming masses and thus to reduce the high cost of living.

It has proposed an amendment to the federal constitution providing for the election of United States senators by the direct vote of the people.

It has secured the admission of Arizona and New Mexico as two sovereign States.

It has required the publicity of campaign expenses both before and after election and fixed a limit upon the election expenses of United States senators and representatives.

It has also passed a bill to prevent the abuse of the writ of injunction.

It has passed a law establishing an eight-hour day for workmen on all national public work.

It has passed a resolution which forced the President to take immediate steps to abrogate the Russian treaty. And it has passed the great supply bills which lessen waste and extravagance and which reduce the annual expenses of the government by many millions of dollars.

We approve the measure reported by the Democratic leaders in the house of representatives for the creation of a council of national defense which will determine a definite naval program with a view to increased efficiency and economy. The party that proclaimed and has always enforced the Monroe doctrine and was sponsor for the new navy, will continue faithfully to observe the constitutional requirements to provide and maintain an adequate and well-proportioned navy sufficient to defend American policies, protect our citizens, and uphold the honor and dignity of the nation.

We denounce the profligate waste of the money wrung from the people by oppressive taxation through the lavish appropriations of recent Republican congresses, which have kept taxes high, and reduced the purchasing power of the people's toil. We demand a return to that simplicity and economy which befits a Democratic government, and a reduction in the number of useless offices, the salaries of which drain the substance of the people.

We favor the efficient supervision and rate regulation of railroads, express companies, telegraph and telephone lines engaged in interstate commerce. To this end we recommend the valuation of railroads, express companies, and telegraph and telephone lines by the interstate commerce commission, such valuation to take into consideration the physical value of the property, the original cost, the cost of reproduction, and any element of value that will render the valuation fair and just.

We favor such legislation as will effectually prohibit the railroads, express, telegraph, and telephone companies from engaging in business which brings them into competition with their shippers; also legislation preventing the overissue of stocks and bonds by interstate railroads, express companies, telegraph and telephone lines and legislation which will assure such reduction in transportation rates as conditions will permit, care being taken to avoid reduction that would compel a reduction of wages, prevent adequate service, or do injustice to legitimate investments.

We oppose the so-called Aldrich monetary bill or the establishment of a central bank, and we believe the people of this country will be largely freed from panics and consequent unemployment and business depression by such a systematic revision of our banking laws as will render temporary relief in localities where such relief is needed, with protection from control or domination by what is known as the "money trust."

Banks exist for the accommodation of the public and not for the control of business. All legislation on the subject of banking and currency should have for its purpose the securing of these accommodations on terms of absolute security to the public and of complete protection from the misuse of the power that wealth gives to those who possess it.

We condemn the present methods of depositing government funds in a few favored banks, largely situated in or controlled by Wall Street, in return for political favors, and we pledge our party to provide by law for their deposit by competitive bidding by the banking institutions of the country, national and State, without discrimination as to locality, upon approved securities and subject to call by the government.

Of equal importance with the question of currency reform is the question of rural credits or agricultural finance. Therefore we recommend that an investigation of agricultural credit societies in foreign countries be made, so that it may be ascertained whether a system of rural credits may be devised suitable to conditions in the United States; and we also favor legislation permitting national banks to loan a reasonable proportion of their funds on real estate security.

We recognize the value of vocational education and urge federal appropriations for such training and extension teaching in agriculture in cooperation with the several States.

We renew the declaration in our last platform relating to the conservation of our natural resources and the development of our waterways. The present devastation of the lower Mississippi Valley accentuates the movement for the regulation of river flow by additional bank and levee protection below, and the diversion, storage and control of the flood waters above and their utilization for beneficial purposes in the reclamation of arid and swamp lands and the development of water-power, instead of permitting the floods to continue, as heretofore, agents of destruction

We hold that the control of the Mississippi River is a national problem. The preservation of the depth of its water for the purpose of navigation, the building of levees to maintain the integrity of its channel and the prevention of the overflow of the land and its consequent destruction, resulting in interruption of interstate commerce, the disorganization of mail service, and the enormous loss of life and property impose an obligation which alone can be discharged by the general government.

We favor the cooperation of the United States and the respective States in plans for the comprehensive treatment of all waterways with a view of coordinating plans for channel improvement with plans for drainage of swamp and overflowed lands, and to this end we favor the appropriation by the federal government of sufficient funds to make surveys of such lands, to develop plans for draining such lands, and to supervise the work of construction.

We favor the adoption of a liberal and comprehensive plan for the development and improvement of our inland waterways with economy and efficiency, so as to permit their navigation by vessels of standard draft.

We favor national aid to State and local authorities in the construction and maintenance of post-roads.

We repeat our declarations of the platform of 1908 as follows:

"The courts of justice are the bulwark of our liberties and we yield to none in our purpose to maintain their dignity. Our party has given to the bench a long line of distinguished justices, who have added to the respect and confidence in which this department must be jealously maintained. We resent the attempt of the Republican party to raise a false issue respecting the judiciary. It is an unjust reflection upon a great body of our citizens to assume that they lack respect for the courts.

"It is the function of the court to interpret the laws which the people enact, and if the laws appear to work economic, social, or political injustice it is our duty to change them. The only basis upon which the integrity of our courts can stand is that of unswerving justice and protection of life, personal liberty, and property. If judicial processes may be abused, we should guard them against abuse.

"Experience has proved the necessity of a modification of the present law relating to injunction and we reiterate the pledges of our platforms of 1896 and 1904 in favor of a measure which passed the United States Senate in 1896, relating to contempt in federal courts and providing for trial by jury in cases of indirect contempt.

"Questions of judicial practice have arisen, especially in connection with industrial disputes. We believe that the parties to all judicial proceedings should be treated with rigid impartiality and that injunctions should not be issued in any case in which an injunction would not issue if no industrial dispute were involved.

"The expanding organization of industry makes it essential that there should be no abridgment of the right of the wage earners and producers to organize for the protection of wages and the improvement of labor conditions, to the end that such labor organizations and their members should not be regarded as illegal combinations in restraint of trade.

"We pledge the Democratic party to the enactment of a law creating a department of labor represented separately in the President's cabinet, in which department shall be included the subject of mines and mining."

We pledge the Democratic party, so far as the federal jurisdiction extends, to an employees' compensation law providing adequate indemnity for injury to body or loss of life.

We believe in encouraging the development of a modern system of agriculture and a systematic effort to improve the conditions of trade in farm products so as to benefit both the consumers and producers. And as an efficient means to this end we favor the enactment by congress of legislation that will suppress the pernicious practice of gambling in agricultural products by organized exchanges or others.

We believe in the conservation and the development for the use of all the people, of the natural resources of the country. Our forests, our sources of water-supply, our arable and our mineral lands, our navigable streams, and all other material resources with which our country has been so lavishly endowed, constitute the foundation of our national wealth. Such additional legislation as may be necessary to prevent their being wasted or absorbed by special or privileged interests should be enacted and the policy of their conservation should be rigidly adhered to.

The public domain should be administered and disposed of with due regard to the general welfare. Reservations should be limited to the purposes which they purport to serve and not extended to include land wholly unsuited therefor. The unnecessary withdrawal from sale and settlement of enormous tracts of public land, upon which tree growth never existed and cannot be promoted, tends only to retard development, create discontent, and bring reproach upon the policy of conservation.

The public land laws should be administered in a spirit of the broadest liberality, towards the settler exhibiting a bona fide purpose to comply therewith, to the end that the invitation of this government to the landless should be as attractive as possible, and the plain provisions of the forest reserve act permitting homestead entries to be made within the national forests should not be nullified by administrative regulations which amount to a withdrawal of great areas of the same from settlement.

We favor legislation so extending or readjusting the payments of water users on the irrigation projects in the arid region as to make the burden of such payments as reasonable as will be consistent with justice and sound policy.

Immediate action should be taken by congress to make available the vast and valuable coal deposits of Alaska under conditions that will be a perfect guaranty against their falling into the hands of monopolizing corporations, associations, or interests.

We believe in fostering by constitutional regulation of commerce the growth of a merchant marine which shall develop and strengthen the commercial ties which bind us to our sister republics of the south, but without imposing additional burdens upon the people and without bounties or subsidies from the public treasury. We urge upon congress the speedy enactment of laws for the greater security of life and property at sea and we favor the repeal of all laws and the abrogation of so much of our treaties with other nations as provide for the arrest and imprisonment of seamen charged with desertion or with violation of their contract of service. Such laws and treaties are un-American and violate the spirit if not the letter of the constitution of the United States.

We favor the exemption from tolls of American ships engaged in coastwise trade passing through the Panama Canal.

We also favor legislation forbidding the use of the Panama Canal by ships owned or controlled by railroad carriers engaged in transportation competitive with the canal.

We reaffirm our previous declarations advocating the union and strengthening of the various governmental agencies relating to pure foods, quarantine, vital statistics, and human health. Thus united and administered without partiality to, or discrimination against, any school of medicine or system of healing, they would constitute a single health service, not subordinated to any commercial or financial interests, but devoted exclusively to the conservation of human life and efficiency. Moreover, this health service should cooperate with the health agencies of our various States and cities without interference with their prerogatives or with the freedom of individuals to employ such medical or hygienic aid as they may see fit.

* *

We reaffirm the position thrice announced by the Democracy in national convention assembled against a policy of imperialism and colonial exploitation in the Philippines or elsewhere. We condemn the experiment in imperialism as an inexcusable blunder which has involved us in enormous expense, brought us weakness instead of strength, and laid our nation open to the charge of abandonment of the fundamental doctrine of self-government. We favor an immediate declaration of the nation's purpose to recognize the independence of the Philippine Islands as soon as a stable government can be established, such independence to be guaranteed by us until the neutralization of the islands can be secured by treaty with other powers. In recognizing the independence of the Philippines our government should retain such land as may be necessary for coaling stations and naval bases.

We welcome Arizona and New Mexico to the

sisterhood of States and heartily congratulate them upon their auspicious beginning of great and glorious careers.

* *

We commend the patriotism of the Democratic members of the senate and house of representatives which compelled the termination of the Russian treaty of 1832, and we pledge ourselves anew to preserve the sacred rights of American citizenship at home and abroad. No treaty should receive the sanction of our government which does not recognize the equality of all our citizens, irrespective of race or creed, and which does not expressly guarantee the fundamental right of expatriation.

The constitutional rights of American citizens should protect them on our borders and go with them throughout the world, and every American citizen residing or having property in any foreign country is entitled to and must be given the full protection of the United States government, both for himself and his property.

We favor the establishment of a parcels-post or postal express and also the extension of the rural delivery system as rapidly as practicable.

We call attention to the fact that the Democratic party's demand for a return to the rule of the people expressed in the national platform four years ago has now become the accepted doctrine of a large majority of the electors. We again remind the country that only by a larger exercise of the reserved power of the people can they protect themselves from the misuse of delegated power and the usurpation of governmental instrumentality by special interest. For this reason the national convention insisted on the overthrow of Cannonism and the inauguration of a system by which United State senators could be elected by direct vote. The Democratic party offers itself to the country as an agency through which the complete overthrow and extirpation of corruption, fraud and machine rule in American politics can be effected.

Our platform is one of principles which we believe to be essential to our national welfare. Our pledges are made to be kept when in office as well as relied upon during the campaign, and we invite the cooperation of all citizens, regardless of party, who believe in maintaining unimpaired the institutions and traditions of our country.

XVI

GOVERNOR WILSON'S SPEECH OF ACCEPTANCE

Mr. Bryan's comments as published on August 9th.

Governor Wilson's speech accepting the Democratic nomination is original in its method of dealing with the issues of the campaign. Instead of taking up the platform plank by plank, he takes the central idea of the Denver platform—an idea repeated and emphasized in the Baltimore platform—and elaborates it, using the various questions under consideration to illustrate the application of the principle. Taking the doctrine that a government is an organization formed for the people themselves and to be perfected by them as an instrument for the accomplishment of such coöperative work as is necessary, he shows how all the evils complained of at the present time grow out of the appropriation by a few of the instrumentalities of government. His speech gives striking evidence of the force of cumulative testimony and also illustrates the power of intelligent analysis. In taking his position so strongly he preempts the ground that Mr. Roosevelt's new party seeks to occupy.

In the course of his argument he indorses the Democratic demand for the popular election of senators, presidential primaries, and "Publicity as to everything that concerns government, from the sources of campaign funds to the intimate debate of the highest affairs of the State." Instead of using epithets and employing denunciation against those who have abused existing systems he seeks reform along rational lines and would cure those defects in governmental forms which have been discovered by experience.

The election of senators by the pople will bring that body within the reach of the voters and convert it from a bulwark of predatory wealth, in which seats have been secured by corrupt means and by the aid of favor-seeking corporations, into a popular body responsive to the people's will. This reform has been described in a former Democratic platform as "the gateway to other reforms" and it would be difficult to overestimate the beneficial effects of this constitutional change.

The presidential primaries which the Baltimore platform indorses, and which Governor Wilson defends, will correct another long-standing and grievous abuse, namely, the selection of presidential candidates in conventions where trading and swapping can defeat the wishes of the people. Ingratitude has been described as a greater sin than revenge, because the former is the repayment of good with ill while the latter is the repayment of ill with ill. We must, therefore, consider at all times the effect of the obligations incurred when so great an honor as the presidency is bestowed upon a public man, however well meaning, by those who may be in control of the convention. It is impossible for a man so nominated and so obligated to give to the public the sort of service that the public has a right to demand. When the presidential primary is adopted in all of the States, as it is quite sure to be within the next four years, the people will be in position to confer the office of chief executive upon the man of their choice and the nominee, being obligated to the people and to the people alone, will rise to the requirements of his high position.

Governor Wilson properly estimates the value of publicity as shown by his sweeping indorsement of the party's position on that subject. The demand for publicity is now so universal that one finds it hard to understand how secrecy could have been tolerated so long; how an intelligent people could have been so slow to recognize that elections and all official service are public affairs.

These three reforms, the popular election of senators, the presidential primaries, and publicity will, in themselves, revolutionize American politics and put the people in control of the federal government.

Governor Wilson devotes considerable time to the tariff question. After announcing that "There should be an immediate revision" and that "it should be downward, unhesitatingly and steadily downward," he proceeds to point out the lines along which reduction should proceed. He says that it should begin with the schedules which have been most obviously used to kill competition and to raise prices in the United States, arbitrarily with regard to the prices pertaining elsewhere in the markets of the world, and that "before it is finished or intermitted it should extend to every item in every schedule which affords any opportunity for monopoly, for special advantage to limited groups of beneficiaries or for subsidized control of any kind in the markets of the country—until special favor of every source shall have been absolutely withdrawn and every part of our laws of taxation shall have been transformed from a system of governmental patronage into a system of just and reasonable charges which shall fall where they will create the least burden." When we shall have done this, he continues, we can fix questions of revenue and business adjustment in a new spirit and with clear minds.

This is a very strong statement of the Democratic position and will commend itself to those who seek the overthrow of the doctrine that protection should be given for protection's sake and the establishment of the doctrine that tariff laws should be framed for the purpose of raising revenues and for that purpose only. He recognizes, and in his speech declares, that there has been no more demoralizing influence in our politics than the idea that "the government is the grand dispenser of favors, the maker and unmaker of fortunes," and he tersely presents the axiomatic truth that favors are never conceived in the general interest, but always for the benefit of the few.

While planting himself firmly upon the principle that tariff laws should be framed for the purpose of collecting revenue, be so framed as to collect revenue with the least hardship and be carried no further than the necessity of the government requires, he approves of the platform declaration that reductions should be made gradually rather than at one stroke.

Governor Wilson deals at some length with the trust question also. He states the conclusions which can now be drawn from experience and asserts an economic truth, namely, that while up to a certain point combinations effect economies in administration and increase efficiency by simplifying and perfecting organization, still that this is true only within limits. It is fortunate for the discussion of the subject that he points out that combination and concentration are not economically beneficial when carried too far. The trust magnates assume that a billion-dollar corporation can produce more economically than a fifty-million-dollar corporation, merely because a fifty-million-dollar corporation may be able to produce more economically than a fifty-thousand-dollar corporation. The socialist makes the same mistake. Both overlook the fact that there is a leak at each step in the descent of authority from the official head of the concern down to the hand of the workman and that, in time, the total leakage overcomes whatever economic advantage there would otherwise be in consolidation.

He states the Democratic position without equivocation or evasion when he declares that he can arrest and prevent monopoly, and that competition can, in a large measure, be revived by changing the laws and forbidding the practises that killed it. The real issue presented by the trust question is whether we shall attempt to restore competition as an effective force or accept the position advanced by socialists and trust magnates, namely, that all competition is hurtful and that monopoly must be accepted as an economic necessity. He takes the Democratic position that monopolies are the result of unwise laws rather than a natural development and that the cure is to be found in the withdrawal of the support which legislation or lack of governmental administrative efficiency has conferred.

In discussing the labor question Governor Wilson has happily protested against the distinctions that have been drawn between the laboring classes and classes described in other ways. He insists that laws that safeguard the lives of laboring men, that improve the physical and moral conditions under which they live and make their hours rational and tolerable, together with the laws that give them freedom to act in their own interest and protect them where they cannot protect themselves —that such laws cannot be properly regarded as class legislation or as anything but measures taken in the interest of the whole people.

Without attempting to outline a plan of currency reform he declares that no mere banker's plan will meet the requirements, no matter how honestly conceived; that it must be a merchants' and farmers' plan as well. This states in another form the doctrine of the Baltimore platform, namely, that banks exist not for the control of commerce, but for the accommodation of the public, and that legislation on this subject should have for its object the securing of these accommodations with protection to the public from the abuse of the power which wealth brings to those who possess it.

Governor Wilson's treatment of the Philippine question will be gratifying to those who have in four campaigns indorsed the Democratic protest against imperialism. He declares that we are not the owners of the Philippine Islands; that we are not even their partners, but that we hold them in trust for the people who live in them.

While the speech of acceptance is not long, it covers a very wide field. The Democratic candidate is in hearty sympathy with the conservation of the nation's resources, with the development of water transportation, with the completion of the canal, with the revival of the merchant marine, and with the extension of postal facilities. He recognizes the importance of health as a national asset and of vocational training for the people. His work as an educator naturally predisposes him to large views on all subjects connected with the separation of the young for the highest usefulness. He is a champion of economy in government; in a word, he believes that the government should not only be conducted by the people but, as would naturally follow, should be conducted in the interest of all the people. Without assuming to formulate a detailed plan for dealing with every condition which may arise, he lifts into a position of supreme importance the dominating thought of the Baltimore platform and appeals to the country for its cooperation in making popular government a reality throughout the land.

XVII

THE INFLUENCE OF MR. BRYAN IN THE CONVENTION

From an article by Joseph L. Bristow, United States Senator from Kansas, published in the New York "World" and St. Louis "Post-Dispatch.

The nomination of Woodrow Wilson by the Democratic convention is the greatest triumph that has come to William J. Bryan in his career, far greater than his first nomination, which was the result of his speech to the Chicago convention. Then the delegates were in condition to be moved by the spectacular demonstration of his oratorical powers. His fight for a progressive platform at St. Louis up to this time probably showed his greatest strength as a tenacious fighter. His nomination for the third time was not opposed seriously, because it was not believed that the Democratic party had a chance for success.

But with flattering prospects this year that the nominee would be elected the enemies of Mr. Bryan's theories of government have made every effort to guard against control of the convention, so that no one in accord with his views and purposes could be nominated. Indeed, it appeared that they had paved an easy way for the nomination of Speaker Clark, but they had not reckoned with the power of Bryan's personality as a delegate in the convention.

For a week I watched closely his masterful hand. Beaten on the first day for temporary chairman by a decisive vote, it clearly appeared that he did not control a majority of the delegates to the convention. His enemies, the reactionaries in the Democratic party, were elated, but Bryan was calm in defeat and confident of ultimate success. He relied on that irresistible influence in American politics, which he termed the "folks at home," but which I shall style public opinion.

No convention or legislative body in this country can stand a great while against concentrated public opinion. And while the reactionary Democrats gnashed their teeth furiously at Bryan, sent forth their prize orators to denounce him, and vented their hatred and anger, insulting remarks and jeers, yet he, in the midst of all the rancorous turmoil, cool and self-possessed, continued with a masterful hand to wield his tremendous power over the convention. He relied with supreme confidence on the force of public opinion to bring the convention to his feet, and he succeeded, in my judgment, beyond his expectations.

Governor Wilson is under obligations to many friends who have worked for his nomination with an ardor that should be exceedingly gratifying to him, yet there is one man whose support and dominating force gave him the nomination, and to-day, towering above other party leaders in American politics, stands the gigantic figure of William J. Bryan.

FROM AN EDITORIAL ARTICLE IN THE NEW YORK "WORLD."

Mr. Bryan was the hero of the Baltimore convention. There can be no doubt of that.

He might have done more, he might have done less and he might have done some things differently, but he is the man who made the fight; he is the man who shaped the issues; he is the man who controlled events.

Whether in all things wisely, whether in all things unselfishly, whether in all things loyally devoted to Governor Wilson, it was his courage, his clearness of vision, his knowledge of the forces with which he had to contend and his splendid mental and physical endurance that gained the day.

We pay this tribute to Mr. Bryan because it is deserved, and we find the more pleasure in it because for many years past there have been occasions almost without number on which we were compelled to disagree with him and to oppose him.

EDITORIAL ARTICLE IN "COLLIER'S WEEKLY."

The service done by Mr. Bryan to his party and the country will not be forgotten. Nobody has in recent years illustrated more wonderfully the truth that the United States is a country in which men often grow surprisingly after they have reached middle life.

Mr. Bryan at Baltimore had all the honesty, courage, and sympathy which have made him leader of the Democratic liberal masses, and he had a maturity, a strength, a distinguished economy of effort, a logic, a control, which marked him as a more formidable and a more complete figure than he has been before in any of his campaigns. We liked the "boy orator" of 1896. We admire and trust the fighting statesman of 1912.

EDITORIAL ARTICLE IN THE WASHINGTON "TIMES."

Mr. Bryan is being credited with having caused all the turmoil that has existed, and still is existing at the Baltimore convention. It is being said that were it not for Bryan the convention would easily have finished its work by Thursday or Friday, and the Democratic party would have entered the campaign united and in perfect harmony.

All of this is true. Had it not been for Mr. Bryan the Democratic party would now be content, but corrupt; harmonious but hypocritical; united, but with the unity of a boss-driven party rather than the unity of a free people acting in promotion of the common good.

When Mr. Bryan appeared on the scene everything was harmonious. The bosses had agreed. There was nothing left for the delegates to do except to serve as a rubber stamp, a phonograph. The same old program had been arranged. Irreconcilable forces were to be placated, apparently. A platform that should be written by the radicals and promising almost anything the people wanted was to be adopted.

The progressives were to be kept in line by the platform promises; the reactionaries were to be kept in line by the secret knowledge that the nominees were perfectly "safe and sane," and could be relied upon not to compel the party to live up to the platform; Mr. Bryan and his ilk were to furnish the oratory and beat the bushes; Mr. Belmont, Ryan, and their ilk were to furnish the money, and ultimately dominate the adminstration. The people were eventually to hold the sack, as they have always done.

Into this very satisfactory harmony program to the bosses and of the bosses, Mr. Bryan threw a bomb. The pieces are still in the air. All that Mr.

Bryan demanded was that cardinal virtue of sincerity. He demanded that if the Democratic party was to make an appeal to the people upon the ground that it was progressive and stood for popular government, that it be a progressive convention from start to finish. He demanded that it be kept free from any obligations to the reactionary element or to the forces of Special Privilege or to the bosses. He demanded that a progressive sound the keynote, a progressive write the platform, and what was of the greatest consequence, a progressive be nominated who would hold the party to its promises, in event it won at the polls.

FROM AN ARTICLE IN "THE NATIONAL MONTHLY," BY NORMAN E. MACK, CHAIRMAN OF THE DEMOCRATIC NATIONAL COMMITTEE.

Bryan's greatest strength in the convention came from the assumption that he was looking for nothing for himself. For four months prior to the convention, he had had under consideration the suggestion that he become temporary chairman of the convention. He had the assurance of the chairman of the national committee that the members of the committee on arrangements would support him for the post if he would indicate a willingness to serve; in fact, there would have been no opposition to Mr. Bryan for temporary chairman, either in the national committee or the convention itself, if he had desired the place and made known his desire prior to the meeting of the arrangement committee in Baltimore who decided the temporary chairmanship in favor of Judge Parker. But Mr. Bryan stated long before that meeting his disinclination to serve. About a month before the convention he sent a letter to the chairman of the national committee, of which the following is a copy:

"Hon. Norman E. Mack, Buffalo, N. Y.:

"My Dear Mack—I wrote you the other day suggesting that the committee should ask the two leading candidates—I suppose they will be Clark and Wilson—to agree upon the temporary chairman. I believe it would be conducive to harmony if we could get a man who would be agreeable to both of these candidates. I neglected to add that I do not desire the position myself. I think that under the circumstances it is better for me not to take a prominent part in the organization of the convention. I suppose I will be a member of the committee on resolutions from this state. I have not conferred with the members of the delegation, but I take it for granted from the personnel that the members of the delegation will favor me for that position.

"Very truly yours,
"W. J. BRYAN."

Nothing could be more conclusive of Mr. Bryan's desire for self-elimination in the bestowal of convention and party honors at Baltimore. Although differing with him as to the selection of the temporary chairman, and the substance of some of his speeches in the convention, we believe it untrue and unfair to put a personal ambition at the base of his fight for a progressive chairman to sound the convention keynote, a progressive candidate and a progressive platform. That he was not plotting for his own nomination is clearly evident. His friends knew that. If there are some who do not believe it to be true, the foregoing letter ought to be a convincing argument.

Part Three

THE PROGRESSIVE NATIONAL CONVENTION
Chicago, August 5-7, 1912

(Note.—It was the original intention of Mr. Bryan to treat in this work only the regular Republican and Democratic conventions. Subsequently he decided to include in the volume the speech of Ex-President Roosevelt before the Progressive convention and the Progressive party platform, with his comments on both, as published in leading daily newspapers immediately following the close of the convention.

It is interesting to note here, as to Mr. Bryan's letters from the Republican convention at Chicago, that, in asking for a ticket for the press gallery, Mr. Bryan promised the Chairman of the National Committee that he would not say anything worse about Mr. Taft and Mr. Roosevelt than they had said about each other; but that understanding would leave him sufficient to say.

Mr. Bryan felt that he was in a position to report the Republican convention with fairness and completeness. He knew both Mr. Taft and Mr. Roosevelt well enough to know what they had said about each other, and he was willing to give it the widest publicity. Mr. Bryan occupied seat Number 13 in the press gallery at the Republican convention, and it was not an unlucky seat either.)

I

A SUMMARY OF EVENTS AT THE CONVENTION

In obedience to the call of the provisional national committee, the first national convention of the Progressive party assembled in Chicago on Monday, August 5, 1912. Albert J. Beveridge, former United States Senator from Indiana, was made temporary chairman without opposition, and O. K. Davis was made secretary. The temporary organization was afterward made permanent. Mr. Beveridge's keynote speech was the only feature of the first day's session.

On Tuesday, the second day, ex-President Roosevelt appeared before the convention by invitation and delivered a speech which was called his "confession of faith." This speech and the platform later adopted agreed almost identically on all important points. Mr. Roosevelt's appearance was the signal for an enthusiastic demonstration which lasted 55 minutes.

In concluding his speech Mr. Roosevelt departed from the original text to explain his attitude toward the colored race, with particular reference to the reasons given for refusing seats as delegates to colored men from the South. He said the southern negro politician had brought about the split in the Republican party, and that the best interests of the colored race could be served by keeping this type of politician out of the councils of the new party.

The report of the committee on credentials, subsequently adopted, barred out colored delegates from southern states.

On Wednesday permanent organization was effected, committees' reports were adopted and the platform accepted without opposition.

Mr. Roosevelt was placed in nomination for the presidency by Comptroller William A. Prendergast of New York City, and seconding speeches were made by a number of persons, including Miss Jane Addams, the Chicago social worker. The nomination by acclamation was made unanimous.

Gov. Hiram Johnson of California was placed in nomination for the vice-presidency by John M. Parker of New Orleans. Judge Ben Lindsey of Denver seconded the nomination and moved that it be made by acclamation. After other seconding speeches had been made, Judge Lindsey's motion was put and carried unanimously.

Mr. Roosevelt and Mr. Johnson were then summoned before the convention and notified of their respective nominations. Amid enthusiasm both accepted in brief but vigorous speeches.

The convention, which had been made unusual by the singing of hymns and patriotic songs, adjourned at 7:24 on Wednesday evening with the singing of the doxology, and a benediction.

II

MR. ROOSEVELT'S SPEECH IN THE CONVENTION

To you, men and women who have come here to this great city of this great State formally to launch a new party, a party of the people of the whole Union, the National Progressive Party, I extend my hearty greeting. You are taking a bold and a greatly needed step for the service of our beloved country. The old parties are husks, with no real soul within either, divided on artificial lines, boss-ridden and privilege-controlled, each a jumble of incongruous elements, and neither daring to speak out wisely and fearlessly what should be said on the vital issues of the day. This new movement is a movement of truth, sincerity, and wisdom, a movement which proposes to put at the service of all our people the collective power of the people, through their governmental agencies, alike in the nation and in the several States. We propose boldly to face the real and great questions of the day, and not skilfully to evade them as do the old parties. We propose to raise aloft a standard to which all honest men can repair, and under which all can fight, no matter what their past political differences, if they are content to face the future and no longer to dwell among the dead issues of the past. We propose to put forth a platform which will not be a platform of the ordinary and insincere kind, but shall be a contract with the people; and, if the people accept this contract by putting us in power, we shall hold ourselves under honorable obligation to fulfil every promise it contains as loyally as if it were actually enforceable under the penalties of the law.

The prime need to-day is to face the fact that we are now in the midst of a great economic evolution. There is urgent necessity of applying both common sense and the highest ethical standard to this movement for better economic conditions among the mass of our people if we are to make it one of healthy evolution and not one of revolution. It is, from the standpoint of our country, wicked as well as foolish longer to refuse to face the real issues of the day. Only by so facing them can we go forward; and to do this we must break up the old party organizations and obliterate the old cleavage lines on the dead issues inherited from fifty years ago. Our fight is a fundamental fight against both of the old corrupt party machines, for both are under the dominion of the plunder league of the professional politicians who are controlled and sustained by the great beneficiaries of privilege and reaction. How close is the alliance between the two machines is shown by the attitude of that portion of those northeastern newspapers, including the majority of the great dailies in all the northeastern cities—Boston, Buffalo, Springfield, Hartford, Philadelphia, and, above all, New York—which are controlled by or representative of the interests which, in popular phrase, are conveniently grouped together as the Wall Street interests.

The large majority of these papers supported Judge Parker for the presidency in 1904; almost unanimously they supported Mr. Taft for the Republican nomination this year; the large majority are now supporting Professor Wilson for the election. Some of them still prefer Mr. Taft to Mr. Wilson, but all make either Mr. Taft or Mr. Wilson their first choice; and one of the ludicrous features of the campaign is that those papers supporting Professor Wilson sow the most jealous partizanship for Mr. Taft whenever they think his interests are jeopardized by the Progressive movement—that, for instance, any electors will obey the will of the majority of the Republican voters at the primaries, and vote for me instead of obeying the will of the Messrs. Barnes-Penrose-Guggenheim combination by voting with it for Mr. Taft.

No better proof can be given than this of the fact that the fundamental concern of the privileged interests is to beat the new party. Some of them would rather beat it with Mr. Wilson; others would rather beat it with Mr. Taft; but the difference between Mr. Wilson and Mr. Taft they consider as trivial, as a mere matter of personal preference. Their real fight is for either as against the Progressives. They represent the allied Reactionaries of the country, and they are against the new party because to their unerring vision it is evident that the real danger to privilege comes from the new party, and from the new party alone. The men who presided over the Baltimore and the Chicago conventions, and the great bosses who controlled the two conventions, Mr. Root and Mr. Parker, Mr. Barnes and Mr. Murphy, Mr. Penrose and Mr. Taggart, Mr. Guggenheim and Mr. Sullivan, differ from one another of course on certain points. But these are the differences which one corporation lawyer has with another corporation lawyer when acting for different corporations. They come together at once as against a common enemy when the dominion of both is threatened by the supremacy of the people of the United States, now aroused to the need of a national alignment on the vital economic issues of this generation.

Neither the Republican nor the Democratic platform contains the slightest promise of approaching the great problems of to-day either with understanding or good faith; and yet never was there greater need in this nation than now of understanding, and of action taken in good faith, on the part of the men and the organizations shaping our governmental policy. Moreover, our needs are such that there should be coherent action among those responsible for the conduct of State affairs; because our aim should be the same in both State and nation; that is, to use the Government as an efficient agency for the practical betterment of social and economic conditions throughout this land. There are other important things to be done, but this is the most important thing. It is preposterous to leave such a movement in the hands of men who have broken their promises as have the present heads of the Republican organizations (not of the Republican voters, for they in no shape represent the rank and file of Republican voters). These men by their deeds give the lie to their words. There is no health in them, and they cannot be trusted.

But the Democratic party is just as little to be trusted. The Underwood-Fitzgerald combination in the House of Representatives has shown that it cannot safely be trusted to maintain the interests of this country abroad or to represent the interests of the plain people at home. The control of the various state bosses in the state organizations has been strengthened by the action at Baltimore; and scant indeed would be the use of exchanging the whips of Messrs. Barnes, Penrose, and Guggenheim for the scorpions of Messrs. Murphy, Taggart, and Sullivan. Finally, the Democratic platform not only shows an utter failure to understand either present conditions or the means of making these conditions better, but also a reckless willingness to try to attract various sections of the electorate by making mutually incompatible promises which there is not the slightest intention of redeeming, and which, if redeemed, would result in sheer ruin. Far-seeing patriots should turn scornfully from men who seek power on a platform which with exquisite nicety combines silly inability to understand the national needs and dishonest insincerity in promising conflicting and impossible remedies.

It seems to me, therefore, that the time is ripe, and overripe, for a genuine Progressive movement, nation-wide and justice-loving, sprung from and responsible to the people themselves, and sundered by a great gulf from both of the old party organizations, while representing all that is best in the hopes, beliefs, and aspirations of the plain people who make up the immense majority of the rank and file of both the old parties.

The first essential in the Progressive program is the right of the people to rule. But a few months ago our opponents were assuring us with insincere clamor that it was absurd for us to talk about desiring that the people should rule, because, as a matter of fact, the people actually do rule. Since that time the actions of the Chicago convention, and to an only less degree of the Baltimore convention, have shown in striking fashion how little the people do rule under our present conditions. We should provide by national law for Presidential primaries. We should provide for the election of United States Senators by popular vote. We should provide for a short ballot; nothing makes it harder for the people to control their public servants than to force them to vote for so many officials that they cannot really keep track of any one of them, so that each becomes indistinguishable in the crowd around him. There must be stringent and efficient corrupt practises acts, applying to the primaries as well as the elections; and there should be publicity of campaign contributions during the campaign. We should provide throughout this Union for giving the people in every State the real right to rule themselves, and really and not nominally to control their public servants and their agencies for doing the public business; an incident of this being giving the people the right themselves to do this public business if they find it impossible to get what they desire through the existing agencies.

I do not attempt to dogmatize as to the machinery by which this end should be achieved. In each community it must be shaped so as to correspond not merely with the needs but with the customs and ways of thought of that community, and no community has a right to dictate to any other in this matter. But wherever representative government has in actual fact become non-representative, there the people should secure to themselves the initiative, the referendum, and the recall, doing it in such fashion as to make it evident that they do not intend to use these instrumentalities wantonly or frequently, but to hold them ready for use in order to correct the misdeeds or failures of the public servants when it has become evident that these misdeeds and failures cannot be corrected in ordinary and normal fashion. The administrative officer should be given full power, for otherwise he cannot do well the people's work; and the people should be given full power over him.

I do not mean that we shall abandon representative government; on the contrary, I mean that we shall device methods by which our Government shall become really representative. To use such measures as the initiative, referendum, and recall indiscriminately and promiscuously on all kinds of occasions would undoubtedly cause disaster; but events have shown that at present our institutions are not representative—at any rate in many States, and sometimes in the nation—and that we cannot wisely afford to let this condition of things remain longer uncorrected. We have permitted the growing up of a breed of politicians who, sometimes for improper political purposes, sometimes as a means of serving the great special interests of privilege which stand behind them, twist so-called representative institutions into a means of thwarting instead of expressing the deliberate and well-thought-out judgment of the people as a whole. This cannot be permitted. * * *

In the contest which culminated six weeks ago in this city I speedily found that my chance was at a minimum in any State where I could not get an expression of the people themselves in the primaries. I found that if I could appeal to the rank and file of the Republican voters, I could generally win, whereas, if I had to appeal to the political caste—which includes the most noisy defenders of the old system—I generally lost. Moreover, I found, as a matter of fact, not as a matter of theory, that these politicians habitually and unhesitatingly resort to every species of mean swindling and cheating in order to carry their point. It is because of the general recognition of this fact that the words politics and politicians have grown to have a sinister meaning throughout this country. The bosses and their agents in the National Republican convention at Chicago treated political theft as a legitimate political weapon. * * *

The American people, and not the courts, are to determine their own fundamental policies. The people should have power to deal with the effect of the acts of all their governmental agencies. This must be extended to include the effects of judicial acts as well as the acts of the executive and legislative representatives of the people. Where the judge merely does justice as between man and man, not dealing with constitutional questions, then the interest of the public is only to see that he is a wise and upright judge. Means should be devised for making it easier than at present to get rid of an incompetent judge; means should be devised by the bar and the bench acting in conjunction with the various legislative bodies to make justice far more expeditious and more certain than at present. The stick-in-the bark legalism, the legalism that subordinates equity to technicalities, should be recognized as a potent enemy of justice. But this is not the matter of most concern at the moment. Our prime concern is that in dealing with the fundamental law of the land, in assuming finally to interpret it, and therefore finally to make it, the acts of the courts should be subject to and not above the final control of the people as a whole. I deny that the American people have surrendered to any set of men, no matter what their position or their character, the final right to determine those fundamental questions upon which free self-government ultimately depends. The people themselves must be the ultimate makers of their own constitution, and where their agents differ in their interpretations of the Constitution the people themselves should be given the chance, after full and deliberate judgment, authoritatively to settle what interpretation it is that their representatives shall therefore adopt as binding. * * *

We in America have peculiar need thus to make the acts of the courts subject to the people, because, owing to causes which I need not now discuss, the courts have here grown to occupy a position unknown in any other country, a position of superiority over both the legislature and the executive. Just at this time, when we have begun in this country to move toward social and industrial betterment and true industrial democracy, this attitude on the part of the courts is of grave portent, because privilege has intrenched itself in many courts, just as it formerly intrenched itself in many legislative bodies and in many executive offices. * * *

I am well aware that every upholder of privilege, every hired agent or beneficiary of the special interests, including many well-meaning parlor reformers, will denounce all this as "Socialism" or "anarchy"—the same terms they used in the past in denouncing the movements to control the railways and to control public utilities. As a matter of fact, the propositions I make constitute neither anarchy nor Socialism, but, on the contrary, a corrective to Socialism and an antidote to anarchy. * * *

In the last twenty years an increasing percentage of our people have come to depend on industry for their livelihood, so that to-day the wage-workers in industry rank in importance side by side with the tillers of the soil. As a people we cannot afford to let any group of citizens or any individual citizen live or labor under conditions which are injurious to the common welfare. Industry, therefore, must submit to such public regulation as will make it a means of life and health, not of death or inefficiency. We must protect the crushable elements at the base of our present industrial structure.

The first charge on the industrial statesmanship of the day is to prevent human waste. The dead weight of orphanage and depleted craftsmanship, of crippled workers and workers suffering from trade diseases, of casual labor, of insecure old age, and of household depletion due to industrial conditions are, like our depleted soils, our gashed mountain-sides and flooded river bottoms, so many strains upon the National structure, draining the reserve strength of all industries and showing beyond all peradventure the public element and public concern in industrial health.

Ultimately we desire to use the Government to aid, as far as can safely be done, in helping the industrial tool-users to become in part tool-owners, just as our farmers now are. Ultimately the Government may have to join more efficiently than at present in strengthening the hands of the workingmen who already stand at a high level, industrially and socially, and who are able by joint action to serve themselves. But the most pressing and immediate need is to deal with the cases of those who are on the level, and who are not only in need themselves, but, because of their need, tend to jeopardize the welfare of those who are better off. We hold that under no industrial order, in no commonwealth, in no trade, and in no establishment should industry be carried on under conditions inimical to the social welfare. The abnormal, ruthless, spendthrift industry of establishment tends to drag down all to the level of the least considerate. * * *

To the first end, we hold that the constituted authorities should be empowered to require all employers to file with them for public purposes such wage scales and other data as the public element in industry demands. The movement for honest weights and measures has its counterpart in industry. All tallies, scales and check systems should be open to public inspection and inspection of committees of the workers concerned. All deaths, injuries, and diseases due to industrial operation should be reported to public authorities.

To the second end, we hold that minimum wage commissions should be established in the nation and in each State to inquire into wages paid in various industries and to determine the standard which the public ought to sanction as a minimum; and we believe that, as a present instalment of what we hope for in the future, there should be at once established in the nation and its several States minimum standards for the wages of women, taking the present Massachusetts law as a basis from which to start and on which to improve. We pledge the Federal government to an investigation of industries along the lines pursued by the Bureau of Mines with the view to establishing standards of sanitation and safety; we call for the standardization of mine and factory inspection by inter-State agreement or the establishment of a Federal standard. We stand for the passage of legislation in the nation and in all States providing standards of compensation for industrial accidents and death, and for diseases clearly due to the nature of conditions of industry, and we stand for the adoption by law of a fair standard of compensation for casualties resulting fatally which shall clearly fix the minimum compensation in all cases.

In the third place, certain industrial conditions fall clearly below the levels which the public to-day sanction.

We stand for a living wage. Wages are subnormal if they fail to provide a living for those who devote their time and energy to industrial occupations. The monetary equivalent of a living wage varies according to local conditions, but must include enough to secure the elements of a normal standard of living—a standard high enough to make morality possible, to provide for education and recreation, to care for immature members of the family, to maintain the family during periods of sickness, and to permit of reasonable saving for old age.

Hours are excessive if they fail to afford the worker sufficient time to recuperate and return to his work thoroughly refreshed. We hold that the night labor of women and children is abnormal and should be prohibited; we hold that the employment of women over forty-eight hours per week is abnormal and should be prohibited. We hold that the seven-day working week is abnormal, and we hold that one day of rest in seven should be provided by law. We hold that the continuous industries, operating twenty-four hours out of twenty-four, are abnormal, and where, because of public necessity or for technical reasons (such as molten metal), the twenty-four hours must be divided into two shifts of twelve hours or three shifts of eight, they should by law be divided into three of eight.

Safety conditions are abnormal when, through unguarded machinery, poisons, electrical voltage, or otherwise, the workers are subjected to unnecessary hazards of life and limb; and all such occupations should come under governmental regulation and control.

Home life is abnormal when tenement manufacture is carried on in the household. It is a serious menace to health, education, and childhood, and should therefore be entirely prohibited. Temporary construction camps are abnormal homes and should be subjected to governmental sanitary regulation.

The premature employment of children is abnormal and should be prohibited; so also the employment of women in manufacturing, commerce, or other trades where work compels standing constantly; and also any employment of women in such trades for a period of at least eight weeks at time of childbirth. * * *

Workingwomen have the same need to combine for protection that workingmen have; the ballot is as necessary for one class as for the other; we do not believe that with the two sexes there is identity of function; but we do believe that there should be equality of right; and therefore we favor woman suffrage. In those conservative States where there is genuine doubt how the women stand on this matter I suggest that it be referred to a vote of the women, so that they may themselves make the decision. Surely if women could vote, they would strengthen the hands of those who are endeavoring to deal in efficient fashion with evils such as the white slave traffic; evils which can in part be dealt with nationally, but which in large part can be reached only by determined local action, such as insisting on the widespread publication of the names of the owners, the landlords, of houses used for immoral purposes. * * *

There is no body of our people whose interests are more inextricably interwoven with the interests of all the people than is the case with the farmers. The Country Life Commission should be revived with greatly increased powers; its abandonment was a severe blow to the interests of our people. The welfare of the farmer is a basic need of this nation. It is the men from the farm who in the past have taken the lead in every great movement within this nation, whether in time of war or in time of peace. It is well to have our cities prosper, but it is not well if they prosper at the expense of the country. I am glad to say that in many sections of our country there has been an extraordinary revival of recent years in intelligent interest in and work for those who live in the open country. In this movement the lead must be taken by the farmers themselves; but our people as a whole, through their governmental agencies, should back the farmers. Everything possible should be done to better the economic condition of the farmer, and also to increase the social value of the life of the farmer, the farmer's wife, and their children. The burdens of labor and loneliness bear heavily on the women in the country; their welfare should be the especial concern of all of us. Everything possible should be done to make life in the country profitable, so as to be attractive from the economic standpoint, and also to give an outlet among farming people for those forms of activity which now tend to make life in the cities especially desirable for ambitious men and women. There should be just the same chance to live as full, as well-rounded, and as highly useful lives in the country as in the city.

The Government must co-operate with the farmer to make the farm more productive. There must be no skinning of the soil. The farm should be left to the farmer's son in better, and not worse, condition because of its cultivation. Moreover, every invention and improvement, every discovery and economy, should be at the service of the farmer in the work of production; and, in addition, he should be helped to co-operate in business fashion with his fellows, so that the money paid by the consumer for the product of the soil shall to as large a degree as possible go into the pockets of the man who raised that product from the soil. * * *

The present conditions of business cannot be accepted as satisfactory. There are too many who do not prosper enough, and of the few who prosper greatly there are certainly some whose prosperity does not mean well for the country. Rational Progressives, no matter how radical, are well aware that nothing the Government can do will make some men prosper, and we heartily approve the prosperity, no matter how great, of any man, if it comes as an incident to rendering service to the community; but we wish to shape conditions so that a greater number of the small men who are decent, industrious and energetic shall be able to succeed, and so that the big man who is dishonest shall not be allowed to succeed at all.

Our aim is to control business, not to strangle it,—and, above all, not to continue a policy of make-believe strangle toward big concerns that do evil, and constant menace toward both big and little concerns that do well. Our aim is to promote prosperity, and then see to its proper division. We do not believe that any good comes to any one by a policy which means destruction of prosperity; for in such cases it is not possible to divide it because of the very obvious fact that there is nothing to divide. We wish to control big business so as to secure among other things good wages for the wage-workers and reasonable prices for the consumers. Wherever in any business the prosperity of the business man is obtained by lowering the wages of his workmen and charging an excessive price to the consumers we wish to interfere and stop such practises. We will not submit to that kind of prosperity any more than we will submit to prosperity obtained by swindling investors or getting unfair advantages over business rivals. But it is obvious that unless the business is prosperous the wage-workers employed therein will be badly paid and the consumers badly served. Therefore not merely as a matter of justice to the business man, but from the standpoint of the self-interest of the wage-worker and the consumer we desire that business shall prosper; but it should be so supervised as to make prosperity also take the shape of good wages to the wage-worker and reasonable prices to the consumer, while investors and business rivals are insured just treatment, and the farmer, the man who tills the soil, is protected as sedulously as the wage-worker himself. * * *

Again and again while I was President, from 1902 to 1908, I pointed out that under the Anti-Trust Law alone it was neither possible to put a stop to business abuses nor possible to secure the highest efficiency in the service rendered by business to the general public. The Anti-Trust Law must be kept on our statute-books, and, as hereafter shown, must be rendered more effective in the cases where it is applied. But to treat the Anti-Trust Law as an adequate, or as by itself a wise, measure of relief and betterment is a sign not of progress, but of toryism and reaction. It has been of benefit so far as it has implied the recognition of a real and great evil, and the at least sporadic application of the principle that all men alike must obey the law. But as a sole remedy, universally applicable, it has in actual practise completely broken down; as now applied it works more mischief than benefit. It represents the waste of effort—always damaging to a community—which arises from the attempt to meet new conditions by the application of outworn remedies instead of fearlessly and in common-sense fashion facing the new conditions and devising the new remedies which alone can work effectively for good. The Anti-Trust Law, if interpreted as the Baltimore platform demands it shall be interpreted, would apply to every agency by which not merely industrial but agricultural business is carried on in this country; under such an interpretation it ought in theory to be applied universally, in which case practically all industries would stop; as a matter of fact, it is utterly out of the question to enforce it universally; and, when enforced sporadically, it causes continual unrest, puts the country at a disadvantage with its trade competitors in international commerce, hopelessly puzzles honest business men and honest farmers as to what their rights are, and yet, as has just been shown in the cases of the Standard Oil and the Tobacco Trust, it is no real check on the great trusts at which it was in theory aimed, and indeed operates to their benefit. Moreover, if we are to compete with other nations in the markets of the world as well as to develop our own material civilization at home, we must utilize those forms of industrial organization that are indispensable to the highest industrial productivity and efficiency. * * *

The Democratic platform offers nothing in the way of remedy for present industrial conditions except, first, the enforcement of the Anti-Trust Law in a fashion which, if words mean anything, means bringing business to a standstill; and, second, the insistence upon an archaic construction of the States' rights doctrine in thus dealing with interstate commerce—an insistence which, in the first place, is the most flagrant possible violation of the Constitution to which the members of the Baltimore convention assert their devotion, and which, in the next place, nullifies and makes an empty pretense of their first statement. The proposals of the platform are so conflicting and so absurd that it is hard to imagine how any attempt could be made in good faith to carry them out; but, if such attempt were sincerely made, it could only produce industrial chaos. Were such an attempt made, every man who acts honestly would have something to fear, and yet no great adroit criminal able to command the advice of the best corporation lawyers would have much to fear.

What is needed is action directly the reverse of that thus confusedly indicated. We Progressives stand for the rights of the people. When these rights can best be secured by insistence upon States' rights, then we are for States' rights; when they can best be secured by insistence upon national rights, then we are for national rights. Interstate commerce can be effectively controlled only by the nation. The States cannot control it under the Constitution, and to amend the Constitution by giving them control of it would amount to a dissolution of the Government. The worst of the big trusts have always endeavored to keep alive the feeling in favor of having the States themselves, and not the nation, attempt to do this work, because they know that in the long run such effort would be ineffective. There is no surer way to prevent all successful effort to deal with the trusts than to insist that they be dealt with by the States rather than by the nation, or to create a conflict between the States and the nation on the subject. The well-meaning ignorant man who advances such a proposition does as much damage as if he were hired by the trusts themselves, for he is playing the game of every big crooked corporation in the country. The only effective way in which to regulate the trusts is through the exercise of the collective power of our people as a whole through the governmental agencies established by the Constitution for this very purpose. * * *

It is utterly hopeless to attempt to control the trusts merely by the Anti-Trust Law, or by any law the same in principle, no matter what the modifications may be in detail. In the first place, these great corporations cannot possibly be controlled merely by a succession of lawsuits. The administrative branch of the Government must exercise such control. The preposterous failure of the Commerce Court has shown that only damage comes from the effort to substitute judicial for administrative control of great corporations. In the next place, a loosely drawn law which promises to do everything would reduce business to complete ruin if it were not also so drawn as to accomplish almost nothing. * * *

What is needed is the application to all industrial concerns and all co-operating interests engaged in interstate commerce in which there is either monopoly or control of the market of the principles on which we have gone in regulating transportation concerns engaged in such commerce. The Anti-Trust Law should be kept on the statute-books and strengthened so as to make it genuinely and thoroughly effective against every big concern tending to monopoly or guilty of anti-social practises. At the same time, a national industrial commission should be created which should have complete power to regulate and control all the great industrial concerns engaged in interstate business—which practically means all of them in this country. This commission should exercise over these industrial concerns like powers to those exercised over the railways by the Interstate Commerce Commission, and over the national banks by the Comptroller of the Currency, and additional powers if found necessary. The establishment of such a commission would enable us to punish the individual rather than merely the corporation, just as we now do with banks, where the aim of the Government is, not to close the bank, but to bring to justice personally any bank official who has gone wrong. This commission should deal with all the abuses of the trusts—all the abuses such as those developed by the Government suit against the Standard Oil and Tobacco Trusts—as the Interstate Commerce Commission now deals with rebates. It should have complete power to make the capitalization absolutely honest and put a stop to all stock watering. Such supervision over the issuance of corporate securities would put a stop to exploitation of the people by dishonest capitalists desiring to declare dividends on watered securities, and would open this kind of industrial property to ownership by the people at large. It should have free access to the books of each corporation and power to find out exactly how it treats its employees, its rivals, and the general public. * * *

Any corporation not coming under the commission should be exposed to prosecution under the Anti-Trust Law, and any corporation violating the orders of the commission should also at once become exposed to such prosecution; and when such a prosecution is successful, it should be the duty of the commission to see that the decree of the court is put into effect completely and in good faith, so that the combination is absolutely broken up, and is not allowed to come together again, nor the constituent parts thereof permitted to do business save under the conditions laid down by the commission. This last provision would prevent the repetition of such gross scandals as those attendant upon the present Administration's prosecutions of the Standard Oil and the Tobacco Trusts. The Supreme Court of the United States in condemning these two trusts to dissolution used language of unsparing severity concerning their actions. But the decree was carried out in such a manner as to turn into a farce this bitter condemnation of the criminals by the highest court in the country. Not one particle of benefit to the community at large was gained; on the contrary, the prices went up to consumers, independent competitors were placed in greater jeopardy than ever before, and the possessions of the wrong-doers greatly appreciated in value. There never was a more flagrant travesty of justice, never an instance in which wealthy wrong-doers benefited more conspicuously by a law which was supposed to be aimed at them, and which undoubtedly would have brought about severe punishment of less wealthy wrong-doers.

The Progressive proposal is definite. It is practicable. We promise nothing that we cannot carry out. We promise nothing which will jeopardize honest business. We promise adequate control of all big business and the stern suppression of the evils connected with big business, and this promise we can absolutely keep. Our proposal is to help honest business activity, however extensive, and to see that it is rewarded with fair returns, so that there may be no oppression either of business men or of the common people. We propose to make it worth while for our business men to develop the most efficient business agencies for use in international trade; for it is to the interest of our whole people that we should do well in international business. But we propose to make those business agencies do complete justice to our own people. * * *

I believe in a protective tariff, but I believe in it as a principle, approached from the standpoint of the interests of the whole people, and not as a bundle of preferences to be given to favored individuals. In my opinion, the American people favor the principle of a protective tariff, but they desire such a tariff to be established primarily in the interests of the wage-worker and the consumer. The chief opposition to our tariff at the present moment comes from the general conviction that certain interests have been improperly favored by overprotection. I agree with this view. The commercial and industrial experience of this country has demonstrated the wisdom of the protective policy, but it has also demonstrated that in the application of that policy certain clearly recognized abuses have developed. It is not merely the tariff that should be revised, but the method of tariff-making and of tariff administration. Wherever nowadays an industry is to be protected it should be on the theory that such protection will serve to keep up the wages and the standard of living of the wage-worker in that industry with full regard for the interest of the consumer. To accomplish this the tariff to be levied should as nearly as is scientifically possible approximate the differential between the cost of production at home and abroad. This differential is chiefly, if not wholly, in labor cost. No duty should be permitted to stand as regards any industry unless the workers receive their full share of the benefits of that duty. In other words, there is no warrant for protection unless a legitimate share of the benefits get into the pay envelope of the wage-worker.

The practise of undertaking a general revision of all the schedules at one time and of securing information as to conditions in the different industries and as to rates of duty desired chiefly from those engaged in the industries, who themselves benefit directly from the rates they propose, has been demonstrated to be not only iniquitous but futile. It has afforded opportunity for practically all of the abuses which have crept into our tariff-making and our tariff administration. The day of the log-rolling tariff must end. The progressive thought of the country has recognized this fact for several years, and the time has come when all genuine Progressives should insist upon a thorough and radical change in the method of tariff-making.

The first step should be the creation of a permanent commission of non-partizan experts whose business shall be to study scientifically all phases of tariff-making and of tariff effects. This commission should be large enough to cover all the different and widely varying branches of American industry. It should have ample powers to enable it to secure exact and reliable information. It should have authority to examine closely all correlated subjects, such as the effect of any given duty on the consumers of the article on which the duty is levied; that is, it should directly consider the question as to what any duty costs the people in the price of living. It should examine into the wages and conditions of labor and life of the workmen in any industry, so as to insure our refusing protection to any industry unless the showing as regards the share labor receives therefrom is satisfactory. This commission would be wholly different from the present unsatisfactory Tariff Board, which was created under a provision of law which failed to give it the powers indispensable if it was to do the work it should do. * * *

As a further means of disrupting the old crooked, log-rolling method of tariff-making, all future revisions of the tariff should be made schedule by schedule as changing conditions may require. Thus a great obstacle will be thrown in the way of the trading of votes which has marked so scandalously the enactment of every tariff bill of recent years. The tariff commission should render reports at the call of Congress or of either branch of Congress and to the President. Under the Constitution, Congress is the tariff-making power. It should not be the purpose in creating a tariff commission to take anything away from this power of Congress, but rather to afford a wise means of giving to Congress the widest and most scientific assurance possible, and of furnishing it and the public with the fullest disinterested information. Only by this means can the tariff be taken out of politics. The creation of such a permanent tariff commission, and the adoption of the policy of schedule by schedule revision, will do more to accomplish this highly desired object than any other means yet devised.

The cost of living in this country has risen during the last few years out of all proportion to the increase in the rate of most salaries and wages; the same situation confronts alike the majority of wage-workers, small business men, small professional men, the clerks, the doctors, clergymen. Now, grave tho the problem is, there is one way to make it graver, and that is to deal with it insincerely, to advance false remedies, to promise the impossible. Our opponents, Republicans and Democrats alike, propose to deal with it in this way. The Republicans in their platform promise an inquiry into the facts. Most certainly there should be such inquiry. But the way the present Administration has failed to keep its promises in the past, and the rank dishonesty of action on the part of the Penrose-Barnes-Guggenheim National Convention, makes their every promise worthless.

The Democratic platform affects to find the entire cause of the high cost of living in the tariff, and promises to remedy it by free trade, especially free trade in the necessaries of life. In the first place, this attitude ignores the patent fact that the problem is world-wide, that everywhere, in England and France, as in Germany and Japan, it appears with greater or less severity; that in England, for instance, it has become a very severe problem, although neither the tariff nor, save to a small degree, the trusts can there have any possible effect upon the situation. In the second place, the Democratic platform, if it is sincere, must mean that all duties will be taken off the products of the farmer. Yet most certainly we cannot afford to have the farmer struck down. The welfare of the tiller of the soil is as important as the welfare of the wage-worker himself, and we must sedulously guard both. The farmer, the producer of the necessaries of life, can himself live only if he raises these necessities for a profit. On the other hand, the consumer who must have that farmer's product in order to live must be allowed to purchase it at the lowest cost that can give the farmer his profit, and everything possible must be done to eliminate any middleman whose function does not tend to increase the cheapness of distribution of the product; and, moreover, everything must be done to stop all speculating, all gambling with the bread-basket which has even the slightest deleterious effect upon the producer and consumer. There must be legislation which will bring about a closer business relationship between the farmer and the consumer. * * *

The effect of the tariff on the cost of living is slight; any householder can satisfy himself of this fact by considering the increase in price of articles, like milk and eggs, where the influence of both the tariff and the trusts is negligible. No conditions have been shown which warrant us in believing that the abolition of the protective tariff as a whole would bring any substantial benefit to the consumer, while it would certainly cause unheard of immediate disaster to all wage-workers, all business men, and all farmers, and in all probability would permanently lower the standard of living here. In order to show the utter futility of the belief that the abolition of the tariff and the establishment of free trade would remedy the condition complained of, all that is necessary is to look at the course of industrial events in England and in Germany during the last thirty years, the former under free trade, the latter under a protective system. During these thirty years it is a matter of common knowledge that Germany has forged ahead relatively to England, and this not only as regards the employers, but as regards the wage-earners—in short, as regards all members of the industrial classes. Doubtless many causes have combined to produce this result; it is not to be ascribed to the tariff alone, but, on the other hand, it is evident that it could not have come about if a protective tariff were even a chief cause among many other causes of the high cost of living.

It is also asserted that the trusts are responsible for the high cost of living. I have no question that, as regards certain trusts, this is true. I also have no question that it will continue to be true just as long as the country confines itself to acting as the Baltimore platform demands that we act. This demand is, in effect, for the States and National Government to make the futile attempt to exercise forty-nine sovereign and conflicting authorities in the effort jointly to suppress the trusts, while at the same time the National Government refuses to exercise proper control over them. There will be no diminution in the cost of trust-made articles so long as our Government attempts the impossible task of restoring the flintlock conditions of business sixty years ago by trusting only to a succession of lawsuits under the Anti-Trust Law—a method which it has been definitely shown usually results to the benefit of any big business concern which really ought to be dissolved, but which cause disturbance and distress to multitudes of smaller concerns. * * *

By such action we shall certainly be able to remove the element of contributory causation on the part of the trusts and the tariff toward the high cost of living. There will remain many other elements. Wrong taxation, including failure to tax swollen inheritances and unused land and other natural resources held for speculative purposes, is one of these elements. The modern tendency to leave the country for the town is another element; and exhaustion of the soil and poor methods of raising and marketing the products of the soil make up another element, as I have already shown. Another element is that of waste and extravagance, individual and national. No laws which the wit of man can devise will avail to make the community prosperous if the average individual lives in such fashion that his expenditure always exceeds his income. * * *

We believe that there exists an imperative need for prompt legislation for the improvement of our national currency system. The experience of repeated financial crises in the last forty years has proved that the present method of issuing, through private agencies, notes secured by Government bonds is both harmful and unscientific. This method was adopted as a means of financing the Government during the Civil War through furnishing a domestic market for Government bonds. It was largely successful in fulfilling that purpose; but that need is long past, and the system has outlived this feature of its usefulness. The issue of currency is fundamentally a governmental function. The system to be adopted should have as its basic principles soundness and elasticity. The currency should flow forth readily at the demand of commercial activity, and retire as promptly when the demand diminishes. It should be automatically sufficient for all of the legitimate needs of business in any section of the country. Only by such means can the country be freed from the danger of recurring panics. The control should be lodged with the Government, and should be safeguarded against manipulation by Wall Street or the large interests. It should be made impossible to use the machinery or perquisites of the currency system for any speculative purposes. The country must be safeguarded against the overexpansion or unjust contraction of either credit or circulating medium.

There can be no greater issue than that of Conservation in this country. Just as we must conserve our men, women, and children, so we must conserve the resources of the land on which they live. We must conserve the soil so that our children shall have a land that is more and not less fertile than that our fathers dwelt in. We must conserve the forests, not by disuse but by use, making them more valuable at the same time that we use them. We must conserve the mines. Moreover, we must insure so far as possible the use of certain types of great natural resources for the benefit of the people as a whole. The public should not alienate its fee in the water power which will be of incalculable consequence as a source of power in the immediate future. The nation and the States within their several spheres should by immediate legislation keep the fee of the water power, leasing its use only for a reasonable length of time on terms that will secure the interests of the people. Just as the nation has gone into the work of irrigation in the West, so it should go into the work of helping reclaim the swamp lands of the South. We should undertake the complete development and control of the Mississippi as a national work, just as we have undertaken the work of building the Panama Canal. We can use the plant, and we can use the human experience, left free by the completion of the Panama Canal, in so developing the Mississippi as to make it a mighty highroad of commerce, and a source of fructification and not of death to the rich and fertile lands lying along its lower length.

In the West, the forests, the grazing lands, the reserves of every kind, should be so handled as to be in the interests of the actual settler, the actual home-maker. He should be encouraged to use them at once, but in such a way as to preserve and not exhaust them. * * *

In international affairs this country should behave toward other nations exactly as an honorable private citizen behaves toward other private citizens. We should do no wrong to any nation, weak or strong, and we should submit to no wrong. Above all, we should never in any treaty make any promise which we do not intend in good faith to fulfil. I believe it essential that our small army should be kept at a high pitch of perfection, and in no way can it be so damaged as by permitting it to become the plaything of men in Congress who wish to gratify either spite or favoritism, or to secure to localities advantages to which those localities are not entitled. The navy should be steadily built up; and the process of upbuilding must not be stopped until—and not before—it proves possible to secure by international agreement a general reduction of armaments. The Panama Canal must be fortified. It would have been criminal to build it if we were not prepared to fortify it and to keep our navy at such a pitch of strength as to render it unsafe for any foreign power to attack us and get control of it. We have a perfect right to permit our coastwise traffic (with which there can be no competition by the merchant marine of any foreign nation—so that there is no discrimination against any foreign marine) to pass through that Canal on any terms we choose, and I personally think that no toll should be charged on such traffic. * * *

The question that has arisen over the right of this nation to charge tolls on the Canal vividly illustrates the folly and iniquity of making treaties which cannot and ought not to be kept. As a people there is no lesson we more need to learn than the lesson not in an outburst of emotionalism to make a treaty that ought not to be, and could not be, kept; and the further lesson that, when we do make a treaty, we must soberly live up to it as long as changed conditions do not warrant the serious step of denouncing it. If we had been so unwise as to adopt the general arbitration treaties a few months ago, we would now be bound to arbitrate the question of our right to free our own coastwise traffic from Canal tolls; and at any future time we might have found ourselves obliged to arbitrate the question whether, in the event of war, we could keep the Canal open to our own war vessels and closed to those of our foes. There could be no better illustration of the extreme unwisdom of entering into international agreements without paying heed to the question of keeping them. On the other hand, we deliberately, and with our eyes open, and after ample consideration and discussion, agreed to treat all merchant ships on the same basis; it was partly because of this agreement that there was no question raised by foreign nations as to our digging and fortifying the Canal; and, having given our word, we must keep it. When the American people make a promise, that promise must and will be kept. * * *

By actual experience in office I have found that, as a rule, I could secure the triumph of the causes in which I most believed, not from the politicians and the men who claim an exceptional right to speak in business and government, but by going over their heads and appealing directly to the people themselves. I am not under the slightest delusion as to any power that during my political career I have at any time possessed. Whatever of power I at any time had, I obtained from the people. I could exercise it only so long as, and to the extent that the people not merely believed in me, but heartily backed me up. Whatever I did as President I was able to do only because I had the backing of the people. When on any point I did not have that backing, when on any point I differed from the people, it mattered not whether I was right or whether I was wrong, my power vanished. I tried my best to lead the people, to advise them, to tell them what I thought was right; if necessary, I never hesitated to tell them what I thought they ought to hear, even though I thought it would be unpleasant for them to hear it; but I recognized that my task was to try to lead them and not to drive them, to take them into my confidence, to try to show them that I was right, and then loyally and in good faith to accept their decision. I will do anything for the people except what my conscience tells me is wrong, and that I can do for no man and no set of men; I hold that a man cannot serve the people well unless he serves his conscience; but I hold also that where his conscience bids him refuse to do what the people desire, he should not try to continue in office against their will. Our Government system should be so shaped that the public servant, when he cannot conscientiously carry out the wishes of the people, shall at their desire leave his office and not misrepresent them in office; and I hold that the public servant can by so doing, better than in any other way, serve both them and his conscience.

Surely there never was a fight better worth making than the one in which we are engaged. It little matters what befalls any one of us who for the time being stand in the forefront of the battle. I hope we shall win, and I believe that if we can wake the people to what the fight really means we shall win. But, win or lose, we shall not falter. Whatever fate may at the moment overtake any of us, the movement itself will not stop. Our cause is based on the eternal principles of righteousness; and even though we who now lead may for the time fail, in the end the cause itself shall triumph. Six weeks ago, here in Chicago, I spoke to the honest representatives of a convention which was not dominated by honest men; a convention wherein sat, alas! a majority of men who, with sneering indifference to every principle of right, so acted as to bring to a shameful end a party which had been founded over half a century ago by men in whose souls burned the fire of lofty endeavor. Now to you men, who, in your turn, have come together to spend and be spent in the endless crusade against wrong, to you who face the future resolute and confident, to you who strive in a spirit of brotherhood for the betterment of our nation, to you who gird yourselves for this great fight in the never-ending warfare for the good of humankind, I say in closing what in that speech I said in closing: We stand at Armageddon, and we battle for the Lord.

III

PLATFORM OF THE PROGRESSIVE PARTY

The conscience of the people, in a time of grave national problems, has called into being a new party, born of the nation's awakened sense of justice.

We of the Progressive party here dedicate ourselves to the fulfilment of the duty laid upon us by our fathers to maintain that government of the people, by the people, and for the people whose foundations they laid.

We hold with Thomas Jefferson and Abraham Lincoln that the people are the masters of their Constitution to fulfil its purposes and to safeguard it from those who, by perversion of its intent, would convert it into an instrument of injustice. In accordance with the needs of each generation the people must use their sovereign powers to establish and maintain equal opportunity and industrial justice, to secure which this government was founded and without which no republic can endure.

This country belongs to the people who inhabit it. Its resources, its business, its institutions, and its laws should be utilized, maintained, or altered in whatever manner will best promote the general interest. It is time to set the public welfare in the first place.

* * *

The deliberate betrayal of its trust by the Republican party and the fatal incapacity of the Democratic party to deal with the new issues of the new time have compelled the people to forge a new instrument of government through which to give effect to their will in laws and institutions. Unhampered by tradition, uncorrupted by power, undismayed by the magnitude of the task, the new party offers itself as the instrument of the people to sweep away old abuses, to build a new and nobler commonwealth.

This declaration is our covenant with the people, and we hereby bind the party and its candidates in State and nation to the pledges made herein.

The National Progressive party, committed to the principle of government by a self-controlled democracy expressing its will through representatives of the people, pledges itself to secure such alterations in the fundamental law of the several States and of the United States as shall insure the representative character of the government.

In particular the party declares for direct primaries for the nomination of State and national officers, for nation-wide preferential primaries for candidates for the presidency, for the direct election of United States Senators by the people, and we urge on the States the policy of the short ballot with responsibility to the people secured by the initiative, referendum and recall.

The Progressive party, believing that a free people should have the power from time to time to amend their fundamental law so as to adapt it progressively to the changing needs of the people, pledges itself to provide a more easy and expeditious method of amending the Federal Constitution.

Up to the limit of the Constitution and later by amendment of the Constitution if found necessary, we advocate bringing under effective national jurisdiction those problems which have expanded beyond reach of the individual States.

It is as grotesque as it is intolerable that the several States should by unequal laws in matters of common concern become competing commercial agencies, barter the lives of their children, the health of their women, and the safety and well-being of their working people for the profit of their financial interests.

The extreme insistence on State's rights by the Democratic party in the Baltimore platform demonstrates anew its inability to understand the world into which it has survived or to administer the affairs of a union of states which have in all essential respects become one people.

The Progressive party, believing that no people can justly claim to be a true democracy which denies political rights on account of sex, pledges itself to the task of securing equal suffrage to men and women alike.

We pledge our party to legislation that will compel strict limitation of all campaign contributions and expenditures, and detailed publicity of both before as well as after primaries and elections.

We pledge our party to legislation compelling the registration of lobbyists; publicity of committee hearings except on foreign affairs and recording of all votes in committee; and forbidding federal appointees from holding office in State or national political organization or taking part as officers or delegates in political conventions for the nomination of elective State or national officials.

The Progressive party demands such restriction of the power of the courts as shall leave to the people the ultimate authority to determine fundamental questions of social welfare and public policy. To secure this end it pledges itself to provide:

(1) That when an act, passed under the police power of the State, is held unconstitutional under the state constitution by the courts the people, after an ample interval for deliberation, shall have an opportunity to vote on the question whether they

desire the act to become law notwithstanding such decision.

(2) That every decision of the highest appellate court of a State declaring an act of the legislature unconstitutional on the ground of its violation of the federal constitution shall be subject to the same review by the Supreme Court of the United States as is now accorded to decisions sustaining such legislation.

The Progressive party, in order to secure to the people a better administration of justice and by that means to bring about a more general respect for the law and the courts, pledges itself to work unceasingly for the reform of legal procedure and judicial methods.

We believe that the issuance of injunctions in cases arising out of labor disputes should be prohibited when such injunctions would not apply when no labor disputes existed.

We also believe that a person cited for contempt in labor disputes, except when such contempt was committed in the actual presence of the court or so near thereto as to interfere with the proper administration of justice, should have a right to trial by jury.

The supreme duty of the nation is the conservation of human resources through an enlarged measure of social and industrial justice. We pledge ourselves to work unceasingly in State and nation for:

Effective legislation looking to the prevention of industrial accidents, occupational diseases, overwork, involuntary unemployment, and other injurious effects incident to modern industry.

The fixing of minimum safety and health standards for the various occupations and the exercise of the public authority of State and nation, including the federal control over interstate commerce and the taxing power, to maintain such standards.

The prohibition of child labor.

Minimum wage standards for working women, to provide for a "living wage" in all industrial occupations.

The general prohibition of night-work for women and the establishment of an eight hour day for women and young persons.

One day's rest in seven for all wage-workers.

The eight hour day in continuous twenty-four hour industries.

The abolition of the convict contract labor system, substituting a system of prison production for governmental consumption only, and the application of prisoners' earnings to the support of their dependent families.

Publicity as to wages, hours, and conditions of labor; full reports upon industrial accidents and diseases and the opening to public inspection of all tallies, weights, measures, and check systems on labor products.

Standards of compensation for death by industrial accident and injury and trade disease which will transfer the burden of lost earnings from the families of working people to the industry and thus to the community.

The protection of home life against the hazards of sickness, irregular employment, and old age through the adoption of a system of social insurance adapted to American use.

The development of the creative labor power of America by lifting the last load of illiteracy from American youth and establishing continuation schools for industrial education under public control and encouraging agricultural education and demonstration in rural schools.

The establishment of industrial research laboratories to put the methods and discoveries of science at the service of American producers.

We favor the organization of the workers, men and women, as a means of protecting their interests and of promoting their progress.

We pledge the party to establish a department of labor with a seat in the cabinet and with wide jurisdiction over matters affecting the conditions of labor and living.

The development and prosperity of country life

are as important to the people who live in the cities as they are to the farmers. Increase of prosperity on the farm will favorably affect the cost of living and promote the interests of all who dwell in the country and all who depend upon its products for clothing, shelter and food.

We pledge our party to foster the development of agricultural credit and cooperation, the teaching of agriculture in schools, agricultural college extension, the use of mechanical power on the farm, and to reestablish the country life commission, thus directly promoting the welfare of the farmers and bringing the benefits of better farming, better business, and better living within their reach.

The high cost of living is due partly to worldwide and partly to local causes; partly to natural and partly to artificial causes. The measures proposed in this platform on various subjects, such as the tariff, the trusts, and conservation, will of themselves remove the artificial causes. There will remain other elements, such as the tendency to leave the country for the city, waste, extravagance, bad system of taxation, poor methods of raising crops, and bad business methods in marketing crops. To remedy these conditions requires the fullest information and, based on this information, effective government supervision and control to remove all the artificial causes. We pledge ourselves to such full and immediate inquiry and to immediate action to deal with every need such inquiry discloses.

* *

We believe that true popular government, justice and prosperity go hand in hand, and, so believing, it is our purpose to secure that large measure of general prosperity which is the fruit of legitimate and honest business, fostered by equal justice and by sound progressive laws.

We demand that the test of true prosperity shall be the benefits conferred thereby on all the citizens, not confined to individuals or classes, and that the test of corporate efficiency shall be the ability better to serve the public; that those who profit by the control of business affairs shall justify that profit and that control by sharing with the public the fruits thereof.

We therefore demand a strong national regulation of interstate corporations. The corporation is an essential part of modern business. The concentration of modern business in some degree is both inevitable and necessary for national and international business efficiency. But the existing concentration of vast wealth under a corporate system, unguarded and uncontrolled by the nation, has placed in the hands of a few men enormous, secret, irresponsible power over the daily life of the citizen—a power insufferable in a free government and certain of abuse.

This power has been abused in monopoly of national resources, in stock-watering, in unfair competition and unfair privileges, and finally in sinister influences on the public agencies of State and nation. We do not fear commercial power, but we insist that it shall be exercised openly, under publicity, supervision, and regulation of the most efficient sort, which will preserve its good while eradicating and preventing its evils.

To that end we urge the establishment of a strong federal administrative commission of high standing, which shall maintain permanent active supervision over industrial corporations engaged in interstate commerce, or such of them as are of public importance, doing for them what the government now does for the national banks and what is now done for the railroads by the interstate commerce commission. Such a commission must enforce the complete publicity of those corporate transactions which are of public interest; must attack unfair competition, false capitalization, and special privilege, and by continuous trained watchfulness guard and keep open equally to all the highways of American commerce.

* *

We pledge ourselves to the enactment of a patent law which will make it impossible for patents to be suppressed or used against the public welfare in the interests of injurious monopolies.

The time has come when the federal government should cooperate with manufacturers and producers in extending our foreign commerce. To this end we demand adequate appropriations by congress and the appointment of diplomatic and consular officers solely with a view to their special fitness and worth and not in consideration of political expediency.

It is imperative to the welfare of our people that we enlarge and extend our foreign commerce. We are preeminently fitted to do this because as a people we have developed high skill in the art of manufacturing. Our business men are strong executives, strong organizers. In every way possible our federal government should cooperate in this important matter.

* *

The natural resources of the nation must be promptly developed and generously used to supply the people's needs, but we cannot safely allow them to be wasted, exploited, monopolized, or controlled against the general good. We heartily favor the policy of conservation, and we pledge our party to protect the national forests without hindering their legitimate use for the benefit of all the people. Agricultural lands in the national forests are and should remain open to the genuine settler. Conservation will not retard legitimate development.

The honest settler must receive his patent promptly without hindrance rules or delays.

We believe that the remaining forests, coal and oil lands, water-powers, and other natural resources still in State or national control (except agricultural lands) are more likely to be wisely conserved and utilized for the general welfare if held in the public hands. In order that consumers and producers, managers and workmen, now and hereafter, need not pay toll to private monopolies of power and raw material, we demand that such resources shall be retained by the State or nation and opened to immediate use under laws which will encourage development and make to the people a moderate return for benefits conferred.

In particular we pledge our party to require reasonable compensation to the public for water-power rights hereafter granted by the public. We pledge legislation to lease to the public grazing lands under equitable provisions now pending which will increase the production of food for the people and thoroughly safeguard the rights of the actual homemaker.

Natural resources whose conservation is necessary for the national welfare should be owned or controlled by the nation.

We recognize the vital importance of good roads, and we pledge our party to foster their extension in every proper way, and we favor the early construction of national highways. We also favor the extension of the rural free delivery service.

The coal and other natural resources of Alaska should be opened to development at once. They are owned by the people of the United States, and are safe from monopoly, waste, or destruction only while so owned. We demand that they shall neither be sold nor given away except under the homestead law, but while held in government ownership shall be opened to use promptly upon liberal terms requiring immediate development.

* *

The rivers of the United States are the natural arteries of this continent. We demand that they shall be opened to traffic as indispensable parts of a great nation wide system of transportation, in which the Panama canal will be the central link, thus enabling the whole interior of the United States to share with the Atlantic and Pacific seaboards in the benefit derived from the canal. It is a national obligation to develop our rivers, and especially the Mississippi and its tributaries, without delay, under a comprehensive general plan governing each river system from its source to its mouth, designed to secure its highest usefulness for navigation, irrigation, domestic supply, water-power, and the prevention of floods.

* *

The equipment, organization, and experience acquired in constructing the Panama canal soon will be available for the lakes to the gulf deep waterway and other portions of this great work, and should be utilized by the nation in cooperation with the various States, at the lowest net cost to the people.

The Panama canal, built and paid for by the American people, must be used primarily for their benefit. We demand that the canal shall be so operated as to break the transportation monopoly now held and misused by the transcontinental railroads by maintaining sea competition with them; that ships directly or indirectly owned or controlled by American railroad corporations shall not be permitted to use the canal, and that American ships engaged in coastwise trade shall pay no tolls.

The progressive party will favor legislation having for its aim the development of friendship and commerce between the United States and Latin American nations.

We believe in a protective tariff which shall equalize conditions of competition between the United States and foreign countries, both for the farmer and the manufacturer, and which shall maintain for labor an adequate standard of living. Primarily the benefit of any tariff should be disclosed in the pay envelope of the laborer. We declare that no industry deserves protection which is unfair to labor or which is operating in violation of federal law. We believe that the presumption is always in favor of the consuming public.

We demand tariff revision because the present tariff is unjust to the people of the United States. Fair dealing toward the people requires an immediate downward revision of those schedules wherein duties are shown to be unjust or excessive.

We pledge ourselves to the establishment of a non-partisan scientific tariff commission, reporting both to the President and to either branch of Congress, which shall report, first, as to the costs of production, efficiency of labor, capitalization, industrial organization and efficiency, and the general competitive position in this country and abroad of industries seeking protection from Congress; second, as to the revenue producing power of the tariff and its relation to the resources of government; and, thirdly, as to the effect of the tariff on prices, operations of middlemen, and on the purchasing power of the consumer.

* *

We condemn the Payne-Aldrich bill as unjust to the people. The Republican organization is in the hands of those who have broken, and cannot again be trusted to keep, the promise of necessary downward revision. The Democratic party is committed to the destruction of the protective system through a tariff for revenue only—a policy which would inevitably produce widespread industrial and commercial disaster. We demand the immediate repeal of the Canadian reciprocity act.

We believe in a graduated inheritance tax as a national means of equalizing the obligations of holders of property to government, and we hereby pledge our party to enact such a federal law as will tax large inheritances, returning to the States an equitable percentage of all amounts collected. We favor the ratification of the pending amendment to the constitution giving the government power to levy an income tax.

* *

We pledge ourselves to a wise and just policy of pensioning American soldiers and sailors and their widows and children by the federal government.

And we approve the policy of the southern states in granting pensions to the ex-confederate soldiers and sailors and their widows and children.

We pledge our party to the immediate creation of a parcels-post, with rates proportionate to distance and service.

We condemn the violations of the civil service law under the present administration, including the coercion and assessment of subordinate employees and the president's refusal to punish such violation after a finding of guilty by his own commission;

his distribution of patronage among subservient congressmen, while withholding it from those who refuse support of administration measures; his withdrawal of nominations from the Senate until political support for himself was secured, and his open use of the offices to reward those who voted for his renomination.

* *

On these principles and on the recognized desirability of uniting the progressive forces of the nation into an organization which shall unequivocally represent the progressive spirit and policy, we appeal for the support of all American citizens, without regard to previous political affiliations.

IV

COMMENTS ON THE PROGRESSIVE PARTY

An article by Mr. Bryan, published in newspapers of Saturday, August 10th.

In considering the new party organized at Chicago under the leadership of ex-President Roosevelt, the subject naturally divides itself into three heads: First, the reason which called the new party into existence; second, its platform of principles; and third, its candidates.

Time alone can tell whether the new organization created for and led by Mr. Roosevelt, is to become a permanent and influential factor in American politics, or merely a temporary protest against the Republican party and its present leadership, and a means of forcing that party to accept the leadership of the progressives.

It may be assumed at the start that to be permanent this must be more than a one-man party. However influential a leader may be, he is hardly large enough to form the foundation of a great party. The mere fact that every man must some time die, precludes the idea of permanence unless the new party has something more enduring to build upon than personality.

Several questions arise, and the answers to them will enable us to form some opinion as to the importance of the new party.

First, would a new party have been organized at this time if Mr. Roosevelt were not a candidate for president? If not, then his ambition to hold the office for a third term is the controlling factor, and no man's ambition is important enough to the public to lead to the formation of a new party. When a real necessity exists for a new party, that necessity will of itself bring forth a new party, and its sponsors will be sufficiently numerous to insure its existence and growth, no matter what may happen to any individual factor in its organization.

Second, would Mr. Roosevelt have favored the organization of a new party had any one beside himself suffered the mortification of defeat at Chicago by President Taft? If he had stayed out of the race and left the field to Senator LaFollette and Senator Cummins, would the defeat of either at the hands of the bosses have furnished him a sufficient reason for leaving the Republican party?

The fact that he refused to take sides between Senator LaFollette and President Taft might justify a negative answer to the above question. The members of the new party may not accept this fact as controlling, but has the character of the Republican party changed materially within the last eight months?

Third: In view of Mr. Roosevelt's denunciation of the Republican party as so boss-ridden as to destroy its usefulness, it may be asked with propriety whether Mr. Roosevelt would have regarded the Republican bosses as an insuperable objection to the party, if he had succeeded in seating enough of his contesting delegates to give him a majority in the convention. If he had controlled the national committee, and it had seated enough of his southern delegates to dominate the convention, would he not now regard the Republican party as a people's party, and the only organization to be trusted?

We see how obnoxious those bosses are, how absolutely destructive the party's usefulness under Mr. Taft's leadership. Would Mr. Roosevelt have been able to neutralize entirely their influence and render them harmless had he succeeded in securing the nomination? Mr. Root's selection as temporary chairman was, of course, made in the interest of the predatory classes, but even after his elevation to that position Mr. Roosevelt continued his efforts to obtain control of the convention.

If he had succeeded, would his success have purged the convention of the evil influence that Mr. Root carried about with him? And, why, except for partisan and personal reasons, does Mr. Roosevelt put the Baltimore convention, which routed the bosses, in the same class with the Chicago convention, which was controlled by the bosses?

These questions are asked because they are pertinent. There is no doubt that the Republican party had done enough to merit defeat. The people have been very lenient with it, but has it forfeited its right to exist? The Republican party cannot hope to continue long upon the stage if a majority of its members rally to the standard of Mr. Roosevelt, but if a majority of the rank and file of the Republican party are reformers, could they not have reorganized and rejuvenated the Republican party from within?

Would not a much larger percentage engage in the work of reorganization than will be willing to leave the party to cast in their lot with a new party? Party ties are strong, and the desertions from Mr. Roosevelt, both in the regular convention and since, show how much easier it is to lead a reform movement within a party than without.

The platform adopted by the new party may be divided into three parts. One part indorses reforms for which the Democratic party has been laboring for years, and, until recently, without much support from those who now hold themselves out as the only ones to be trusted with the securing of remedial legislation.

The labor bureau, for instance, with a seat in the cabinet, is a thing for which the Democratic party has been contending, also the election of senators by direct vote, and direct primaries.

Our Baltimore platform was the first national platform to demand presidential primaries, and it went beyond the platform of the new party in demanding the popular election of national committeemen and a change in the system whereby a national committeeman will begin to serve as soon as elected, thus creating a new committee for the preliminary work of each convention.

A considerable part of the labor plank is taken from previous Democratic platforms. It is ungrateful in the new party to accuse our party of "total incapacity," while using our material.

A part of the platform deals with state issues, such planks, for instance, as those favoring the initiative, the referendum, the recall, and woman suffrage. These propositions are before the people in a number of States, and the indorsement of them will, of course, strengthen them, but it has not been customary for national platforms to deal with subjects which were not before congress, or connected with the work of the national administration.

A part of the new section of the platform is commendable. For instance, the demand for a constitutional amendment making easier and more expeditious the amending of the federal constitution.

We need such an amendment, and the people will welcome any assistance that the new party may be able to give this movement.

The planks in regard to the conservation of human resources will appeal to the public, especially those prohibiting child labor and excessive hours, together with those demanding a day of rest each week, a living minimum wage, legislation for the prevention of accidents, for the abolition of convict contract labor and for publicity in regard to labor conditions.

The inheritance tax plank is also good, and the plank calling for greater safeguards for the prevention of monopoly of our national resources.

The tariff plank is the same old sham that has been used for a generation. The protective system is held up as a sacred institution and support is given to the tariff commission idea, which is always brought forward to delay reduction.

The plank on the trust question is a restatement of Mr. Roosevelt's position which leads directly to socialism. The doctrine that the trust is a natural development and must be accepted as permanent is the basis of the socialist propaganda.

The socialist, however, recognizes that a private monopoly cannot be successfully controlled, and insists that the government shall own and operate the trusts. The new party, on the other hand, clings to the idea that the trusts can be left in private hands and yet be effectively controlled through a national bureau.

All history is against this theory. Municipalities are taking over municipal plants because city councils are corrupted by municipal corporations. If it is impossible for a municipal plant to be successfully controlled when in private hands, how can we hope to control billion-dollar trusts through a national bureau when the trusts will have so large a pecuniary interest in controlling the administration that appoints the members of the bureau?

The position of the new party on the trust question is so absolutely untenable as to prevent its indorsement by any large number of the people.

The most Rooseveltesque plank of the platform, however, is the one demanding an indefinite extension of the powers of the federal government and the abridgment of the rights of the States. This has for years been the dominant note in Mr. Roosevelt's political creed. The restraints of the constitution are irritating to him.

He not only desires to enlarge the authority of the federal government at the expense of the state, but he desires to enlarge the powers of the national executive at the expense of the other departments. Whatever Democrats may think of Mr. Roosevelt's attitude on other questions, and however highly they may regard the national work he has done, they cannot join him in overturning the constitutional division of authority between state and nation.

The Democratic party believes in the full use of federal authority for the protection of the public, but instead of substituting federal remedies for state remedies, it would add federal remedies to state remedies, and thus give the people the benefit of both. The Roosevelt plan, however honestly advanced, is not in the interest of popular government, but in the interest of a more selfish and sordid exploitation of the people.

Every lawyer knows that the big corporations fly to the federal courts to escape state courts.

And now, as to the candidates:

Governor Johnson, the nominee for vice-president, is an excellent man, and has made a splendid record as a progressive, but the fact that Mr. Roosevelt was the only one considered in connection with the presidential nomination, shows how completely the organization is based upon him and his personality.

Conceding everything that can be said in behalf of his great ability, his fighting qualities, and his educational work, it must not be forgotten that he has his weaknesses, that he is human.

If it is true, as has been widely circulated, that some progressive—Hadley or Cummins, for instance —could have been nominated instead of Mr. Taft, but for Mr. Roosevelt's refusal to give way, then this must in itself weigh strongly in the minds of many earnest and honest progressives.

If he could have secured the nomination of some one in harmony with his views upon a platform reasonably progressive, and thus thrown a united party behind a Republican progressive and a progressive platform—if he could have done this—many Republicans against whose motives he can bring no just accusation will feel that he did not exhaust all efforts within the party before starting out to disrupt the organization to which he is indebted for all of his prominence and influence.

Mr. Roosevelt will also have to meet the question raised as to his tardiness in espousing the reforms which he now advocates. Democrats, at least, will feel that a party which, like the Democratic party, has been fighting in behalf of reforms for many years ought to receive some consideration from one who has violently opposed, as Mr. Roosevelt has, many radical reforms when the Democratic party was making great sacrifices in their behalf.

Why, for instance, should a Democrat leave the Democrat party, which has labored in behalf of the popular election of senators for 20 years, in behalf of an income tax for 18 years, for railroad regulation for 16 years, for antitrust legislation for 12 years, for publicity, before the election, as to campaign contributions for four years and for

THE CANDIDATE WE ALL SUPPORT.
(*De Mar in the Philadelphia "Record."*)

tariff reform for a generation; why should a Democrat leave such a party to march under the leadership of a commander who did not begin advocating the popular election of senators until two years ago, the income tax until about six years ago, railroad regulation until less than eight years ago, has remained silent during all these years as to tariff extortion and has in every campaign since 1892 joined Wall Street, the subsidized press, the plunderbund and the bosses in defeating the Democratic party?

Assuming that his conversion is sincere, why does he not bring forth works meet for repentance instead of demanding the chief seat at the feast? He ought not to slander the party that has furnished him nearly every reform that he has espoused.

A third objection that he must prepare to meet is that founded upon his position on the trust question. He failed for seven years and a half while President to check or even control the trusts; he has not only kept silent for 11 years while the Steel Trust has exploited the country, but he permitted the Steel Trust to swallow up its largest rival, and he now accepts a Steel Trust director as his chief financial backer and advocates federal incorporation, the very thing that the trusts have clamored for for a generation.

A fourth, and the greatest objection, is his desire for a third term, an honor declined by Washington and Jefferson, and withheld from Grant. A third term opens the door to any number of terms. What emergency requires it? The tendency is toward a single term, not toward a third term.

A president wields more power than any king or emperor or czar, and his power increases each year. Surely the hatred of the progressive Republicans toward the Democratic party is as implacable as it is impossible to explain it, if they are willing to risk the dangers of an unlimited succession of presidential terms rather than use the Democratic party, with its progressive platform and progressive ticket, to rebuke the Republican party for failing to keep step with the progressive spirit of the age.

POLITICS AND PEOPLE

The Ordeal of Self-Government in America

An Arno Press Collection

Allen, Robert S., editor. **Our Fair City.** 1947

Belmont, Perry. **Return to Secret Party Funds:** Value of Reed Committee. 1927

Berge, George W. **The Free Pass Bribery System:** Showing How the Railroads, Through the Free Pass Bribery System, Procure the Government Away from the People. 1905

Billington, Ray Allen. **The Origins of Nativism in the United States, 1800-1844.** 1933

Black, Henry Campbell. **The Relation of the Executive Power to Legislation.** 1919

Boothe, Viva Belle. **The Political Party as a Social Process.** 1923

Breen, Matthew P. **Thirty Years of New York Politics, Up-to-Date.** 1899

Brooks, Robert C. **Corruption in American Politics and Life.** 1910

Brown, George Rothwell. **The Leadership of Congress.** 1922

Bryan, William Jennings. **A Tale of Two Conventions:** Being an Account of the Republican and Democratic National Conventions of June, 1912. 1912

The Caucus System in American Politics. 1974

Childs, Harwood Lawrence. **Labor and Capital in National Politics.** 1930

Clapper, Raymond. **Racketeering in Washington.** 1933

Crawford, Kenneth G. **The Pressure Boys:** The Inside Story of Lobbying in America. 1939

Dallinger, Frederick W. **Nominations for Elective Office in the United States.** 1897

Dunn, Arthur Wallace. **Gridiron Nights:** Humorous and Satirical Views of Politics and Statesmen as Presented by the Famous Dining Club. 1915

Ervin, Spencer. **Henry Ford vs. Truman H. Newberry:** The Famous Senate Election Contest. A Study in American Politics, Legislation and Justice. 1935

Ewing, Cortez A.M. and Royden J. Dangerfield. **Documentary Source Book in American Government and Politics.** 1931

Ford, Henry Jones. **The Cost of Our National Government:** A Study in Political Pathology. 1910

Foulke, William Dudley. **Fighting the Spoilsmen:** Reminiscences of the Civil Service Reform Movement. 1919

Fuller, Hubert Bruce. **The Speakers of the House.** 1909

Griffith, Elmer C. **The Rise and Development of the Gerrymander.** 1907

Hadley, Arthur Twining. **The Relations Between Freedom and Responsibility in the Evolution of Democratic Government.** 1903

Hart, Albert Bushnell. **Practical Essays on American Government.** 1893

Holcombe, Arthur N. **The Political Parties of To-Day:** A Study in Republican and Democratic Politics. 1924

Hughes, Charles Evans. **Conditions of Progress in Democratic Government.** 1910

Kales, Albert M. **Unpopular Government in the United States.** 1914

Kent, Frank R. **The Great Game of Politics.** 1930

Lynch, Denis Tilden. **"Boss" Tweed:** The Story of a Grim Generation. 1927

McCabe, James D., Jr. (Edward Winslow Martin, pseud.) **Behind the Scenes in Washington.** 1873

Macy, Jesse. **Party Organization and Machinery.** 1912

Macy, Jesse. **Political Parties in the United States, 1846-1861.** 1900

Moley, Raymond. **Politics and Criminal Prosecution.** 1929

Munro, William Bennett. **The Invisible Government** and **Personality in Politics:** A Study of Three Types in American Public Life. 1928/1934 Two volumes in one.

Myers, Gustavus. **History of Public Franchises in New York City,** Boroughs of Manhattan and the Bronx. (Reprinted from **Municipal Affairs,** March 1900) 1900

Odegard, Peter H. and E. Allen Helms. **American Politics:** A Study in Political Dynamics. 1938

Orth, Samuel P. **Five American Politicians:** A Study in the Evolution of American Politics. 1906

Ostrogorski, M[oisei I.] **Democracy and the Party System in the United States:** A Study in Extra-Constitutional Government. 1910

Overacker, Louise. **Money in Elections.** 1932

Overacker, Louise. **The Presidential Primary.** 1926

The Party Battle. 1974

Peel, Roy V. and Thomas C. Donnelly. **The 1928 Campaign:** An Analysis. 1931

Pepper, George Wharton. **In the Senate** *and* **Family Quarrels:** The President, The Senate, The House. 1930/1931. Two volumes in one

Platt, Thomas Collier. **The Autobiography of Thomas Collier Platt.** Compiled and edited by Louis J. Lang. 1910

Roosevelt, Theodore. **Social Justice and Popular Rule:** Essays, Addresses, and Public Statements Relating to the Progressive Movement, 1910-1916 (*The Works of Theodore Roosevelt,* Memorial Edition, Volume XIX) 1925

Root, Elihu. **The Citizen's Part in Government** *and* **Experiments in Government and the Essentials of the Constitution.** 1907/1913. Two volumes in one

Rosten, Leo C. **The Washington Correspondents.** 1937

Salter, J[ohn] T[homas]. **Boss Rule:** Portraits in City Politics. 1935

Schattschneider, E[lmer] E[ric]. **Politics, Pressures and the Tariff:** A Study of Free Private Enterprise in Pressure Politics, as Shown in the 1929-1930 Revision of the Tariff. 1935

Smith, T[homas] V. and Robert A. Taft. **Foundations of Democracy:** A Series of Debates. 1939

The Spoils System in New York. 1974

Stead, W[illiam] T. **Satan's Invisible World Displayed,** Or, Despairing Democracy. A Study of Greater New York (The Review of Reviews Annual) 1898

Van Devander, Charles W. **The Big Bosses.** 1944

Wallis, J[ames] H. **The Politician:** His Habits, Outcries and Protective Coloring. 1935

Werner, M[orris] R. **Privileged Characters.** 1935

White, William Allen. **Politics:** The Citizen's Business. 1924

Wooddy, Carroll Hill. **The Case of Frank L. Smith:** A Study in Representative Government. 1931

Wooddy, Carroll Hill. **The Chicago Primary of 1926:** A Study in Election Methods. 1926